Daily Habits to Learnza

A book on 365 daily habits for mindfulness, meditation, and success

by

Hamza Haqqi

First Edition: May 2021
Printed in the United States of America
ISBN: [9798746444714]

"To those learners who, in spite of everything, still struggle, fight, and remain positive this book is dedicated to you"

Table of Contents

Acknowledgement

This book is dedicated to the teams at Learnza, LLC and Learnza PK. Their hard-work and dedication daily does not go unnoticed since it is commendable for them to follow this dream and vision set in motion 5 years ago. This book acknowledges their efforts and struggles in the realm of academics post Covid-19 pandemic. Their sacrifices are noticed since they are constantly fighting for educational equality.

Prologue

Mentor was the son of Heracles and Asopis in Greek mythology. Mentor was an old acquaintance of Odysseus, who had left Mentor and Odysseus' foster-brother Eumaeus in possession of his son Telemachus, as well as Odysseus' palace, when Odysseus left for the Trojan War.

Flashforward to 2021 taking Greek Mythology to the modern day Learnza, LLC a developmental and psychological based company started as an idea of mentorship in building the mentor and mentee relationship. It has evolved from necessary academic coaching to life coaching and career coaching. Currently, Learnza is opening its doors to students facing challenges in an all-online curriculum to help blend learning and increase student awareness and retention on the issue that they are facing both academically and personally.

Learnza is a web-based life coaching and mentoring company that aims to meet the need for timely academic assessments of students while providing teaching, thereby avoiding lost teaching time, and the theme of a creating a shared vision, and Learnza uses this influence to improve high test scores on high-stakes test

Learnza bridges the gap between academics and life coaching, and the mentor/mentee relationship. The COVID-19 Pandemic has created more disconnects in academics and the already fragile academic environment both in person and digitally. The students cannot build professional relationships with their teachers in the digital format and are bombarded with endless assignments and tasks. The goal of learning is to help create more mindful students in a holistic learning environment that blends Gerontology, Academics, and Psychology. Learnza refers to this as (GAP). Thus, we use the GAP method to fill in the gap in learning and create students who value lifelong education.

Learnza is an urban tutoring and academic research company, not a chain tutoring company. Other tutoring companies in the DFW area are solely for profit and pray on the community's misinformation regarding high-stakes testing. They overcharge for materials, exams and teach large classes online.

Learnza always teaches one-on-one in a holistic educational environment. They are promoting wellness and mindfulness: all materials, exams, and even keto-friendly vegan snacks. Learnza helps show students and families the value of life coaching in academics. We join you to visit Learnza.com likewise students enrolled at Learnza actively help the research community learn about the dangers of burnout in an increasingly digital format of high-school post-COVID-19 pandemic. These high-stakes tests cause insufficient self-esteem, inducing burnout, fatigue, exhaustion, and long-term mental health issues. All this can be overwhelming for students and families. Thus, the team of tutors and mentors, and life coaches at Learnza, LLC help teach SAT/ACT and college preparatory curriculum along with valuable life skills. Visit us at LEARNZA.COM to learn more about what Learnza can do for you? This book is dedicated to the students, families, and tutors that represents Learnza what it is today. Along with purchase of this book proceeds go to Camp Learnza initiative which helps rural children all over the world in developing countries learn and grow and fight child labor.

Chapter 1

Introduction to Daily Habits to Mindfulness (365 Days Plan)

My parents taught my brother and I about mindfulness and me when growing up, but that was not the word they used. We practiced the reverence of the five daily prayers by folding our arms, sitting quietly, and patiently listening. Growing up was quiet, and the patient was a struggle. I wrestled with my mind and body in those moments, reflecting. I wanted to do anything else but sit still, but sit still, I certainly did...... most of the time. Praying five times a day was a way to challenge my mind and heart, but I managed to see the beauty in the stillness and thank my mother and father everyday for instilling in my brother and me the values of faith, family, forgiveness. Thus, The Daily Habits to Mindfulness chapter is a methodological approach based on the TCA approach at Learnza. The TCA approach used at Learnza LLC, this systematic and methodological approach guides my teaching, practice, and this book. approach to learning takes the term, applies the concept, and gives a practical application.

Practicing reverence as a child led me to commit my life to the practice and study of mindfulness. Again, growing up was not easy in Omaha, Nebraska. I was a petite, scrawny Muslim boy with an ambition that stretched as high as my imagination. I started my first meditation group in high-school, and then, in my early 20s, I had the great privilege of opening my heart and mind to our wonderful concepts of corporate and educational wellness through motivational and educational coaching. Learnza LLC was the brainchild of years of struggling to find the career and faith I was seeking. It is the combination of “learning” with “Hamza” which was at the forefront of how Learnza came into existence. The humble days of tutoring out of a Starbucks to offices in Dallas boomed in to offices in Omaha, San Diego, and most recently Manhattan. I grew and so did the impact and journey to promote motivational coaching and mindfulness mindset. Flashforward, after founding

Learnza LLC, consulting with schools, yoga and meditation studios, leading corporate training on mindfulness, and working with influencers, celebrities, politicians, and executives became a daily occurrence. The objective again was on training minds and bodies to achieve their ultimate goals and potential and practice among a daily routine.

Furthermore, these years of hands-on experience, combined with the life coaching I've enjoyed working on Learnza, LLC with students, combined with dedicated practices and an insatiable thirst for truth, justice, and equality. This inspired me to write my doctoral thesis at Baylor University, *"A Phenomenal Study to Understand the Impact of Motivational Coaching on Students' Lived Experiences at an Urban Tutoring Academy."* Again, the goal of daily mindfulness, mediation, and reflection is critical to the DNA of both Learnza and you, the reader.

Furthermore, establishing a daily mindfulness practice is a powerful decision. Just five minutes a day of meditation for a year has no incredible effects and takes practically no time at all. I am excited to share this 365-day guide to meditation to support you in your commitment to daily mindfulness practice. Through this book, I will support you in every single way possible. First, set it up like a calendar, beginning January 1 and ending December 31. The book will include some of the most effective mindfulness exercises, meditations, affirmations, mantras, and inspirational quotes that I have found useful in my journey and mindfulness practices. You can open these pages to the appropriate date and dive right into a relaxing and rewarding mindfulness practice. There is no right or wrong way to start your daily habits to Learnza. Trust yourself, trust the process and keep the faith. The motivation will come from within you to do amazing things once you can visualize the goal.

According to research, mindfulness practices can specifically increase feelings of calm and relaxation even in the face of stressful situations, giving you more energy and clarity to face life's challenges. The subtle relationship between you and your mind and body will strengthen with the consistent practice presented in this book, and you will adopt a more confident, accepting, compassionate, and wise perspective.

Thus, incorporating daily mindfulness exercise into your life delivers numerous benefits to your relationships, work, finances, and physical well-being. When practicing mindfulness, you may also find your intuition, attention to detail, and ability to return and process information increase dramatically.

Again, throughout the book, you will encounter various meditations, exercises, and mantras that speak to developing and growing from mindfulness practice. Certain practices will be done sitting up, standing, and others lying down. Some will incorporate physical movement like walking or eating, and others will utilize movement in the body to balance mind/body coordination and left/right brain with you throughout your day, a perspective to adopt, or an affirmation to use. Use these as you go about your day and as stressors arise.

(You'll notice that the affirmations are written in the present progressive tense, which helps guide the mind away from current thought patterns and toward a new perspective.) Mantra, which means "meditation object," is a word, phrase, sound, object, or idea that serves as a reference point in meditation. Find your mantra and keep it close to your heart as you embark on this journey. Also, when reading, take some time to reflect. There is no A+ in mindfulness; you must go about your day with peace and faith, allowing your mind to wander if it so desires.

When the mind wanders, we bring it back to the mantra. Several of the mantras included in this book are written in Latin. The purpose of having the mantra in Latin is that this is a dead language. Occurring as no one's normal conversational language means that fewer mental associations will come up as you use it. Each mantra is explained as to its meaning and purpose along the journey in *Daily Habits to Learnza.*

This book is an excellent tool in your arsenal for taking great care of yourself, psychological and mental well-being, and establishing a greater sense of well-being. However, if you are experiencing any ongoing or debilitating sadness, anxiety, or feelings of depression, this book is not a replacement for a therapist or proper medical attention. There is no shame in seeking help or treatment, and while this book will help navigate the tumult of everyday living, a professional should address more extreme cases. Seek medical attention if causes of depression manifest or worsen.

You are about to embark on a subtle but compelling path of developing your mind and soul powers. Be gentle with yourself. Let go of any sense of strain, and allow this to be simple, rich, and nourishing. This is both good for you and good for everyone who comes into contact with you. The more you practice, the more you will notice the transformational healing effects of mindfulness in your life, including increased patience, increased passion and enthusiasm, reduced stress, and increased creativity and critical thinking. Remember it is only through practice you will achieve perfection. Affirm and believe in a better and stronger version of yourself.

Enjoy the process!

Trust the process!

Have faith in the process!

- Hamza Haqqi -

Let's begin!

Chapter 2

Daily Habits to Mindfulness (365 Days Plan)

DAY 1

TABULA RASA

Today is full of new possibilities. Meditate for at least five minutes silently repeating the mantra "Tabula Rasa'' which means "blank slate" This is the start of the new year and a new you! When the mind wanders, come back to the mantra. With each exhale, allow a wave of relaxation to pass through the body, as if it's swiping the slate clean and begin a new!

DAY 2

ZEN

Practice the Zen means using the discipline or breath awareness meditation, referred to as zazen.

This is a "sealed mediation" position and wonderful tool in your arsenal.

1. Sit in a comfortable position and allow the body to become still.

2. Close your eyes and bring your inner awareness to the breath.

3. Focus on the breath, the stillness. Notice the sensations of the breath.

4. Become aware of any thoughts or images that may arise in the mind, always bringing the awareness back to the breath. Use the concept of Zen in your own daily practices. As you start framing your intention for the start of the year.

DAY 3

THE SILVER LINING

Cultivate the attitude of a positive onlooker by offering sincere compliments to everyone you meet. Embrace a relaxed sense of positivity. Ask yourself, *"What is something good, beautiful, or praiseworthy about this person?"* Let them know what you think. Let them feel your positivity. Every cloud has a beautiful silver lining.

If you're ever going to find a silver lining

It's gotta be a cloudy day

If you wanna fill your bottle up with lightning

You're gonna have to stand in the rain

- Kacey Musgrave -

DAY 4

SELF-PERCEPTION PRACTICE

Learn to see yourself in a new way. Today's meditation will help you experience your own facial features through your sense of touch.

1. Close your eyes and sit relaxed and comfortably.

2. Allow every muscle in your body to relax and become still be one with the idea of you.

3. With one hand, begin to feel the surface of your own face slowly and gently, touching

your forehead, hairline, eyebrows, closed eyelids, cheekbones, nose, jawline and lips.

4. Notice the various textures

5. Acknowledge that I am unique and beautiful with all my perfect imperfections.

DAY 5

INVOKING EPIPHANY

Open your mind to seeing things differently by practicing mindful observation. Glance around not excluding or focusing on anything in particular, and silently say to yourself *"The more I see, the more I begin to see"* When your gaze rests upon one object, repeat the mantra and allow your gaze to move to another object. Practice this for at least five minutes allowing openness.

DAY 6

OPEN AWARENESS

Mindfulness is the total awareness of all your senses.

1. Find a comfortable Place to sit and practice open awareness

2. Close your eyes

3. Bring your awareness to your breathing

4. Mentally scan the environment around you

5. Notice the subtle sounds and movement all around you, as if you are sitting the eye of the storm resting in your own peaceful space.

DAY 7

AFFIRMATION FOR RESILIENCE

"The only constant is change-- I am naturally very resilient, stronger, and determined repeat 5 times.

DAY 8

PERPETUAL MOTION

Practice seeing everything as a process in the perpetual motion of its own life cycle rather than as a stationary object suspended in time. Life in constant motion experience every second.

DAY 9

BODY ACTIVATION

Awaken every aspect of your body today with a standing mindful self-massage.

1. Massage each finger of both hands.
2. Encircle the wrists and stretch the fingers
3. Massage the muscles in the forearms, and move upward to the bicep, triceps and deltoid muscles of both arms.
4. Roll your shoulders three times backward and three times forward.
5. Lean your chin to your chest and slowly roll your neck all the way around to the left and to the right three times each.
6. Twist your spine by turning the body from the waist up to the left and then to the right. Repeat three times.

7. Fold forward to massage your left and right thigh muscles and then your left and right calf muscles.

8. Stand tall, lifting each foot and rotating your ankle three times in each direction.

9. Finally, close your eyes and allow your arms to rest to either side, taking three deep breaths.

DAY 10

THE UNIFIED FIELD

Envision an invisible field of energy connecting everyone and everything together. As we breather, we draw upon the same life force energy that all other things draw upon.

DAY 11

GOOD VIBES

Practice an audible mantra meditation to focus your attention on the vibration of sound itself.

1. Sit in a comfortable position and allow the body to relax.

2. Set a timer for five minutes.

3. With every exhale, release a gentle humming sound “mmm…”

4. Make sure to keep your attention on the physical experience of the mantra rather than the sound.

5. Continue humming with every exhale until your timer goes off.

DAY 12

HONESTY

On a clean sheet of paper, write a deeply honest letter to someone with whom you have difficulty. Write with compassion and wisdom, apologizing for any misdeeds on your end and being very clear about any mistakes you believe they made against you. AS you write it, breather through the emotions and feelings that may come up, clearing through any old resentment and releasing it entirely.

Sign the letter and when you are finished, tear it up and throw it away.

DAY 13

ORDER IS DIVINE

It is said that *"cleanliness is next to godliness, and order is divine"*

Throughout your day today, practice creating order. The ancient practice of feng shui is the technique observing elemental energy flow through different environments, such as the workplace, home, and garden. Lt your personal world become a little more divine by cleaning out your closet, organizing your desk, or detailing your car.

DAY 14

MASTERING YOUR AGENDA

Take a moment to reflect on all the commitments, goals, or obligations you may have today.

1. Close your eyes, get into a comfortable position, and set a timer for at least five minutes.

2. Allow every exhale to bring a wave of relaxation through all the muscles in the body.

3. Reflect on the day ahead, morning, afternoon, and evening. Visualize the different meetings or encounters that may happen.

4. Breather through them and consider the best possible outcomes

5. Know that the best outcomes you imagine now may not play out exactly as you plan

6. Notice the different thoughts and ideas that come to mind.

7. Send positivity to every person, environment, and circumstance that may arise.

8. At the end of the day today, reflect on how things went

DAY 15

BRIGHT TOMORROW

When our days become dreary with low-hovering clouds of despair, and when our nights become darker than a thousand midnights, let us remember that there is a creative force in this universe working to pull down the gigantic mountains of evil, a power that is able to make a way out of no way and transform dark yesterdays into bright tomorrows.

--Martin Luther King Jr.

DAY 16

LITTLE BY LITTLE

Today, be as present as possible when it comes to your personal goals. Make small changes and stay committed to yourself, especially in the challenging moments. Cultivate momentum by performing the actions that connect you to your goals. What are three things you can do today that will take you one step closer to them?

DAY 17

SHOWER MEDITATION

Bring mindfulness into your routine. Allow the rain to shower you.

When the sun shines, we will shine together
Told you I'll be here forever
Said I'll always be your friend
Took an oath, I'm stick it out 'til the end

Now that it's raining more than ever
Know that we'll still have each other
You can stand under my umbrella
You can stand under my umbrella

- Rihanna

DAY 18

THIS IS YOUR WORLD

This meditation is intended to deepen your connection to the world around you and to cultivate a sense of ownership over the reality that we are all co creating.

1. Begging your meditation by setting a timer for five minutes or more and getting into a comfortable position.

2. Silently repeat the statement, *"The world belongs to the living as I live, the world belongs to me"*

3. When your timer goes off, stretch the body in any way that feels comfortable for you.

4. Take a deep breath and say out loud, *"The world belongs to the living as I live, the world belongs to me"*

5. Today notice the different things you see throughout the world. This is your world. Are you happy with how society operates? Are you comfortable with the social order that you observe?

DAY 19

AFFIRMATION FOR CALMNESS

"I am capable of cultivation calmness and peace even in the face of challenges great and small"

DAY 20

BREAKTHROUGH

Sometimes in life, we can feel stuck. This might show up as a sense of hopelessness or depression, or a worry that we may never be free from a certain problem. In these circumstances, we need breakthroughs.

Focus on the following mantra *"Breakthrough is coming"*

Notice the thoughts that arise in the mind, especially thoughts pertaining to any of your particular concerns or areas of uncertainty.

Always return to the mantra *"Breakthrough is coming"*

DAY 21

BODY OF LIGHT

1. Lie down flat on your back with your palms facing up.

2. On your inhale, breather in and direct the air into the top and the button, the left and the right, and the frog and the back sides of the lungs.

3. On your exhale, breather out from the top and the bottom, the left and the right, the front and the back sides of the lungs.

4. Envision your inhale delivering light throughout your nervous system.

5. Envision your exhale amplifying the light and shining it in all directions around you.

DAY 22

SOCIAL AGREEMENT INSIGHT MEDITATION

Society is a system of agreements among individuals and the larger group. Many of these agreements are conscious, while many are unconscious. This meditation will open your mind to seeing the social agreements you participate in both consciously and unconsciously.

1. Take a seat in a comfortable position and set a timer for at least five minutes.

2. Close your eyes and bring awareness to your breath.

3. Silently ask yourself, *"What have I agreed to?"*

4. Observe the thoughts that arise in your mind and breather through them.

5. Repeat the question as a mantra *"What have I agreed to?"*

6. Release any sense of judgement, simply witness the thoughts and ideas your mind naturally presents.

7. Continue to repeat the question as a mantra *"What have I agreed to?"*

8. When your timer goes off, take a few deep breaths.

9. Journal any particular insight that may arise.

DAY 23

CONSCIOUS EVOLUTION

Reflect on your habits, decisions, and behaviors. Practice asking yourself, *"Does this support the life I am trying to create?"*

DAY 24

MEDITATION ON SOUND

Take a moment for meditation now.

1. Sit and begin by listening

2. Imagine that you can feel every sound you hear in all directions around you.

3. In your mind's eye, "see" the sound waves as they move through the atmosphere.

4. Allow your attention to centralize itself on your breath while holding an open awareness that fills your surroundings.

As you go about your day, become mindful of the various sounds you hear. Notice the subtle sounds you make. Do so without judgement of yourself or others, practice nonattachment, allowing everything to be exactly as it is.

DAY 25

NEW DAY< NEW LIFE

Every day is a new life to an enlightened person. Move through your day as if you are experiencing everything for the very first time.

Try to see the world with fresh eyes.

DAY 26

SO HAPPY AND GRATEFUL

Gratitude unlocks new possibilities. Today, you will practice being grateful for the things you have.

1. Have a seat, close your eyes, and take a few deep breaths. Set a timer for at least five minutes and relax.

2. Take a mental inventory of all that you're grateful for, especially things that you may usually overlook.

3. When the timer goes off, make a list, itemizing everything you're grateful for, using the structure *"I am so happy and grateful for…."*

DAY 27

AFFIRMATION FOR NON-ATTACHMENT

"Today, I would practice letting go of ties to consequences, seeing both outcomes as experiences for the life-learning journey. I am thankful for all of the lessons I have experienced. I am thankful that I am continuing to read, and I am certain that any and all results will be used to my advantage and learning."

-Hamza Haqqi

DAY 28

20 SECOND BREATH

1. Conscious meditation will help to relax an overactive mind and immerse you in the current moment.

2. Practice a 5-5-5-5 Breath for five minutes.

3. Breathe in for five seconds

4. Hold the breath for five seconds.

5. Breathe out for five seconds

6. Hold the empty lungs for five seconds

7. Repeat

DAY 29

SHARPENING THE AXE

"If I had six hours to chop down a tree, I would spend the first four hours sharpening the axe"

- Abraham Lincoln -

DAY 30

SPIRIT OF GENEROSITY

Generosity does not become activated once we have excess. It is a quality of the spirit that is unrelated to one's resources. Generosity can be expressed in kindness, warmth, loving words, kind notes, and many other ways in addition to the generous giving of material resources.

1. Set a timer, for at least five minutes and settle into a comfortable position.

2. Envision yourself as a dignified, confident and generous person.

3. Notice if your posture changes as you breather and embody the qualities of dignity, confidence and generosity.

4. First, ask yourself, *"In what ways am I already generous?"*

5. Notice the memories that come to mind.

6. Then ask yourself, *"In what ways can I be generous today?"*

7. Observe the ideas that arise.

8. When you finish your meditation, make an effort to take action on these new ideas. Practice generosity in one form or another today.

DAY 31

AFFIRMATION FOR WISDOM

"Every day and in every way, I increase in knowledge and understanding"

DAY 32

THE MATURE MIND

As we mature, we are initiated into deeper dimensions of understanding. A mature psyche knows that the quality of their character and the depth of their fulfilment in connection with others are more important than appearances.

Reflect honestly in meditation on the ways you have been mature and the ways you have been immature. Breathe through anything that comes up, loving and accepting yourself exactly where you are in your process while holding space for yourself to continue to mature in the ways you are ready to.

DAY 33

GRACE AND FLOW

Grace is the universe's way of keeping things moving even when things aren't going well. Consider how a river gradually but steadily cuts its way through a mountain over time. Use the mantra "I move with grace; I go with the flow" throughout your day today. Say it silently in your head and aloud whenever a problem arises.

DAY 34

THE PHYSICAL MECHANISM

Our physical bodies are capable of navigating the majority of situations on their own. For example, in most cases, the lungs breathe without conscious effort, the heart beats on its own, and various other organs function without our knowledge. Simply experience the body succeeding on its own in your meditation practice today. Take five minutes to reflect and observe the body as it goes through its various processes.

DAY 35

MIND AND MOUTH

Bring mindfulness into your dental hygiene in this toothbrushing meditation.

1. Begin by noticing the taste inside your mouth.

2. Run your tongue along the surface of your teeth, the from the back, and biting surfaces of both the top and bottom rows of teeth.

3. Do this slowly and feel every single tooth with your tongue.

4. Now begin to brush. Do so slowly and become very conscious of the way you are brushing.

5. Close your eyes and envision the bristles as you feel them along your teeth and gums.

6. Brush your tongue, the roof of your mouth, your gums, and even the inside of your cheeks. Do this slowly and meditatively, being very present with the experience,

7. Bring consciousness into your rinse as well. Notice the experience and take your time.

DAY 36

MINDFUL SMELLING

Olfactory senses hold deep memories and meaning. Breathe in and out through your nose, paying attention to the sensations you feel as the air moves in and out. What are you smelling? Is it bringing back any memories? What emotions does it elicit in you?

Practice mindful check-ins throughout the day and pay attention to the smells you encounter in the environments you pass through.

DAY 37

YOUNG AT ANY AGE

"We carry with us the burden of what thousands of people have said and the memories of all our misfortunes. To abandon all that totally is to be alone, and the mind that is alone is not only innocent but young-- not in time or age, but young innocent, alive at whatever age-- and only such a mind can see that which is truth and that is not measurable by words"

- Jiddu Krishnamurti -

DAY 38

YOUR RELATIONSHIP WITH MONEY

Take at least five minutes to practice meditation reflecting on your relationships with money in order to practice non-attachment, non-judgement, and mindful observation.

1. Get into a comfortable position, set a timer, and close your eyes.

2. Bring your awareness to the breath and allow every exhale to bring relaxation, decompression and self-acceptance.

3. Let go of any anxiety, fear, worry, or ambition. Just be present.

4. Ask yourself, *"What characterizes my relationship with money?"*

5. Observe the thoughts that automatically arise in response to the question.

6. Ask again, *"What characterizes my relationship with money?"*

7. Maintain non-judgement and non-attachment. Continue breathing, Continue asking yourself the same question and observing the thoughts and ideas that arise.

DAY 39

SELF-ACCEPTANCE

Lie down flat on your back with your hands relaxed and resting over your heart center. Silently repeat the mantra, *"I am what I am, and that's all that I am."* Allow yourself to become aware of and let go of unnecessary expectations you may have of yourself. Practice this for at least 3-5 minutes today.

DAY 40

VISUALIZATION FOR PERFECT HEALTH

Visualization uses our "inner eye" to conceptualize something we would like to see or experience with our "outer eyes". Practice visualization meditation specifically for physical health and healing today.

1. Have a seat with your spine erect, each vertebra stacked upon one another.

2. Rest comfortably sitting up, with the balance of the bones holding the body up, allowing the muscles to relax.

3. In your mind's eye, visualize your body healthy and strong.

4. Envision any wounds or illnesses clearing out and being replaced with perfectly functioning cells and tissues.

5. "See" your muscles becoming stronger and more toned.

6. Cultivate a feeling of joy, happiness, and enthusiasm for your physical well-being.

7. Appreciate your body exactly as it is, loving as it is, knowing that the body is always changing.

8. Envision the body simply getting healthier and stronger.

DAY 41

AFFIRMATION FOR POWER

"My strength emerges spontaneously through my true self, not from coercion."

-Hamza Haqqi

DAY 42

LOVE AND ACCEPTANCE

Self-acceptance is the gateway to genuine acceptance of others. Of course, we always want to improve, heal, and grow, but we may never achieve perfection in every area, so it can be very transformational to practice learning to love something that is "imperfect".

In your journal or on a clean sheet of paper, take a few minutes to write using the following formula.

"Even though love and accept myself completely I knowledge that I am not perfect and I'm never going to be perfect for perfection is an unrealistic expectation."

When you finish, take a few deep breaths before moving on with your day.

DAY 43

HOPE

Allow your mind to be open to the constructive unfolding of life. Develop a sense of optimism because, even in the midst of overwhelming odds, a positive result is always probable.

DAY 44

LIGHTNESS OF BEING

1. There are many circumstances of life that may seem daunting. This meditation will assist you in experiencing the sensation of being both anchored and weightless at the same time.

2. Sit comfortably, allowing your back to be erect with your hands open in your lap, palms up.

3. Bring your awareness to your breath.

4. Notice the thoughts that through your mind.

5. Allow yourself to soften and relax, feeling held in place by gravity.

6. Let go of any tension held anywhere in the body, each exhale bringing a wave of decompression through every muscle group.

7. Observe the experience of heaviness that holds the body to the floor with the exhale.

8. Allow every inhale to bring a sense of expansion, breathing in deeply, expanding the lungs in all directions.

9. Observe the experience of lightness with the inhale.

10. Allow the body to be very still, if possible, allowing the only movement in the body to be the breath and the heartbeat.

DAY 45

AFFIRMATION FOR LOVE AND JOY

"This is a loving world working toward my highest evolution. I was made to feel the full range of emotions, and my creator bestowed upon me the divine force of free will. I've been asked to choose passion and joy, and I've accepted. Today, I choose joy and love."

DAY 46

BREAKING GENERATIONAL CURSES

In several respects, we are the beneficiaries to an exceptional inheritance, a planet full of amazing technologies, sophisticated infrastructure, and great knowledge. Among other respects, we've inherited curses that have hampered us for centuries. It is up to the living to destroy the curses by being mindful of them and breaking them.

DAY 47

MINDFUL EATING

Make your meals your meditation. Mindful eating is about fully experiencing the food as you eat and eating foods that will nourish and strengthen your body.

1. Before eating, take a moment for gratitude, appreciating everything on your plate.

2. Eat one bite at a time, putting the fork down between bites.

3. Chew slowly and notice the flavors and textures inside your mouth.

4. Mentally "follow" the food as you swallow it, feeling it move into your stomach.

5. Notice the way the food makes you feel before, during and after you eat.

6. Do not rush

DAY 48

CLEAR THE CLUTTER

Non-Attachment has many forms-- letting go of the need for specific outcomes, releasing unnecessary physical possessions, and maintaining healthy relationship dynamics, to name a few.

Minimalism is one way of practicing non-attachment to physical possessions.

Look around your home, car, or office today. Is there clutter? Are you holding on to things you really don't need? Consider choosing a few things to give away, donate, or recycle as an act of non-attachment.

DAY 49

THERE IS SO MUCH MORE

Throughout your day, open your awareness to all that surrounds you, We take so many things for granted. As you observe the world today, silently repeat the following mantra. *"There is so much more to know about that_______"* Name specific things you see, whether it be a chair, a person, a cloud, a tree and so on.

DAY 50

AHHH...THANK YOU. YES!

This meditation-- amplified and activated through your sincerity of intent-- will help you embody and experience a genuine sense of happiness and gratitude.

1. Get into a comfortable position and set a timer for at least five minutes.

2. Open your mind to being genuinely grateful, not for anything in particular.

3. Close your eyes and bring your awareness to your breath.

4. On your exhales, silently repeat the mantra "Ahhh...Thank you. Yes!"

5. When your timer goes off, sigh out the mantra out loud three times.

DAY 51

WE ARE ONE

Among the world's many spiritual traditions, there are many different teachings that can lead us to greater understanding and acceptance of others. In the Eastern traditions, this is communicated in the great adage "we are one". In the Western traditions, we hear of everyone being brothers and sisters.

Meditate on the following mantra to draw you close to other members of the human family.

"Everything and everyone is connected. If it's happening anywhere to anyone, it's happening to me"

DAY 52

MIRROR GAZING

In the yogic traditions, there is a practice called Taraka, wherein the meditator gazes directly into the flame of a candle in an open eye meditation practice. For this mindfulness exercise, you will be gazing into your own eyes in the mirror.

1. Sit or stand comfortably in front of a mirror and set a timer for five or more minutes.

2. Gaze directly into the reflection of your own eyes.

3. Allow all the muscles in your face and shoulders to relax and soften under their own weight.

4. When your gaze moves from the reflection of your own eyes, bring it back.

5. Observe the thoughts, emotions, or physical sensations that may arise.

DAY 53

ACCOUNTABILITY AND RESPONSIBILITY

Taking responsibility for our character defects communicates to our unconscious minds that things need to change from the inside out.

Reflect on a personal situation that feels uncomfortable or unresolved for you.

1. Write an objective description of what happened and try to be as fair as possible when describing it. No one will read this but you.

2. In what ways did you contribute to the rift or negativity of the situation?

3. What could you have done differently?

4. What will you do next time something similar takes place?

DAY 54

SKIN DEEP BODY-SCAN

Scan your awareness along the surface of your skin across your entire body in this meditation.

1. Become still and bring your awareness to the surface of your skin across your entire body.

2. Notice the parts of your body where there is clothing resting.

3. Bring your awareness to the parts of the body anchored to the ground by gravity.

4. Observe the different areas of your skin and get the slightly different experiences they are all having.

5. Practice an open awareness of the entire surface area of the body at once.

DAY 55

AFFIRMATION FOR PEACE

"I can create peace by being peaceful"

DAY 56

YOUR PSYCHIC FORCE FIELD

Humans have an inherent connection to all that surrounds us, we can identify as "empaths". It can be easy to get caught up in the emotional or physical experiences of those around us, and while empathy is a powerful tool for loving and supporting others. It's important that we know where our emotions are coming from.

Sometimes what you're feeling doesn't even belong to you.

Imagine yourself surrounded by an invisible energetic sphere of protection. Move throughout your day as if you carry with you this force field that repels negative energy.

DAY 57

TO GIVE IS TO RECEIVE

Anything we give physically, we no longer hold. Anything we give metaphysically we increase. When we give positivity, we receive more positivity. When we offer negativity, we receive more negativity. Let today be about positivity. Throughout your day, silently use the mantra, "To give is to receive".

DAY 58

PATTERN DISRUPTION

Have you noticed the same problems happening again and again?

We tend to repeat history until we learn the lesson it's trying to teach us. Pay close attention today to any patterns or dynamics that seem familiar-- is there a new way these situations can be navigated?

What can you learn from them?

DAY 59

PURE CONSCIOUSNESS

Meditation is the dissolution of thoughts in Eternal Awareness or Pure Consciousness without objectification, knowing without thinking, merging finitude in infinity.

-Voltaire

DAY 60

Levitation Meditation

Have some fun with this deeply healing levitation meditation.

1. Set a timer for at least five minutes, longer if you're not an experienced levitator.

2. Lie down flat on your back with your palms facing up.

3. On your inhale, breather into the top and the bottom, the left and the right, the front and the back sides of the lungs.

4. On your exhale, breathe out from the top and the bottom, the left and the right, the front and the back sides of the lungs.

5. Envision your inhale gently lifting your body off the ground as you levitate comfortably in the air.

6. Allow your exhale to deepen the stillness and relaxation felt throughout your body.

DAY 61

TERRA FIRMA

When we are emotionally triggered, we can have a positive reaction. This mantra will help you get back on track. Set a timer for at least five minutes, relax quietly, shut your eyes, and softly repeat the mantra "Terra Firma," which translates to "firm earth." Pay careful attention to the areas of your body that are held in place by gravity. Take note of the emotions that emerge, returning your attention to the mantra "Terra Firma" at all times.

DAY 62

TENSEGRITY

The propagation of stress or problems within a community or network is referred to as tensegrity. The general belief is that when tension, threats, or difficulties are spread equally, they are easier to handle. What forms would you be of use to someone now to assist them in dealing with their difficulties? How do you share and process your personal problems with others so that they become more manageable?

DAY 63

NAMASTE

Namaste is one of the most famous and commonly used yogic expressions. It means *"the life within me recognizes the life within you"* or *"the divine within me honors the divine within you"*

Throughout your day, notice every single living being you encounter and take a moment to inwardly bow to them by silently saying the word namaste. Notice the deepened sense of respect and connection that may arise.

DAY 64

YOUR EPIC MYTH

Every superhero and sage has their own unique origin story, spiritual gifts, and superpowers. No two are exactly alike. Reflect on your true life circumstances as if they were part of an epic myth of an incredible world changer. What are your gifts and powers? What problems do you solve?

DAY 65

WALKING MEDITATION

With open eyes, practice walking as a meditation, this can be done in your home, on the sidewalk, or at a park.

1. Walk at a pace a little slower than a usual walk.

2. When you step with your left foot, silently say “Stepping left”

3. When you step with your right foot, silently say “Stepping right”

4. Hold your hands between your sternum and your navel with your elbows bent and fingers interlaced.

5. Keep your head and eyes forward, noticing the sights and sounds in your periphery.

DAY 66

AFFIRMATION FOR PROGRESS

"I seek and strive for progress in my life. I do not need or expect perfection"

DAY 67

MINDFUL LISTENING

Let today be about mindful listening. Ask open-ended questions and listen intently to the answers. We often think about what we will say next while the other person is talking, notice when your mind does this, breather through it, and come back to mindful listening.

Take in what is being said. Take a few breaths to allow their words to sink in before responding.

DAY 68

LOVINGKINDNESS

Practice a loving-kindness meditation.

1. Get into a comfortable position and set your timer for five or more minutes.

2. Sit and silently say to yourself, *"I am here to experience happiness and joy, I am here to experience connection and love. I am here to experience health and vitality'"*

3. Bring to mind close loved ones and silently say to them, *"You are here to experience happiness and joy. You are here to experience connection and love. You are here to experience health and vitality"*.

4. Now envision your friends and neighbors, coworkers, colleagues, and acquaintances, silently telling them the same statements,

5. Next, bring to mind those with whom you have difficulty, offering them the same statements.

6. Finally, send the same message to all the world while envisioning people from all walks of life, plants, animals, the earth itself and all the cosmos.

DAY 69

AFFIRMATION FOR TRUTH SEEKERS

"There is no end to the mysteries of the universe, but I will continue to seek the truth wherever it may be. I count myself among the truth seekers receiving the gifts of knowledge passed down from previous generations to benefit from"

DAY 70

SELF-COMPASSION BODY SCAN

Lovingkindness meditations are a powerful way to cultivate compassion, receive it for ourselves, and direct it to others. Today, practice a lovingkindness body scan meditation, directing love, acceptance, and compassion to every part of your body.

1. Lie down comfortably on your back, in loose-fitting clothing.

2. Close your eyes and bring your awareness to the breath.

3. Mentally scan every part of your body, beginning with your head and moving all the way down to your feet.

4. Visualize a warm glow or light filling each body part as you silently say, *"Thank you, I love you, you are perfect."*

DAY 71

PSYCHIC DIET

Everything we experience enters into our psyche as data. Then our unconscious mind processes that information and makes subtle adjustments to the way we see the world.

Today, notice what data you are filling your psyche with-- this is your "psychic diet." From the music you listen to, to the programs you watch, all are sending subtle messages to your unconscious mind.

Ask yourself.

1. What symbols am I taking in?
2. What does my psychic diet consist of?
3. What messages am I allowing myself to receive?

DAY 72

OPEN EYE MEDITATION

Today, we will practice open-eye meditation. It can be very powerful to cultivate the ability to experience meditative consciousness with our eyes open because most of the challenges we face in our lives occur when our eyes are wide open.

1. Get into a comfortable position and set a timer for at least five minutes.

2. Choose a point on the wall on which to rest your gaze.

3. Bring your inner awareness to your breath, allowing each exhale to bring a wave of relaxation through every part of the body.

4. Notice when your gaze moves from the original gazing point and bring it back.

5. Allow all the muscles in the body to rest under their own weight.

6. Observe the different thoughts and feelings that arise, always keeping the gaze on the original gazing point.

DAY 73

EVERYDAY MIRACLES

All in the world starts inside and radiates outward, and wonders are no exception. Today, we will be receptive to witnessing wonders everywhere about us, as well as a change in mindset from terror to love. In meditation and during the day, silently recite the same mantra to yourself.

"I am willing to believe in miracles. I am willing to see it better, to see compassion instead of this."

DAY 74

AFFIRMATION FOR JOY

"I can chose pleasure even in the face of the most difficult trials."

DAY 75

SMILE IT OUT ☺

1. Face nerves are closely attached to areas of the brain that signal chemical releases correlated with various emotions.

2. When we smile, we naturally release a mixture of "happy" chemicals into our bodies. Today, practice a breath awareness meditation while smiling, encouraging every muscle in your body to relax except for the huge smile.

3. Get comfortable, set your timer for at least five minutes, close your eyes, and smile.

4. Bring awareness to your breath, allowing each exhale to send a wave of relaxation through every part of the body.

5. Allow only the muscles in the face associated with a smile to be activated everything else should rest under its own weight.

6. Notice how you feel and what thoughts, images, ideas, feelings or sensations arise. Observe them with non-attachment.

DAY 76

MEDITATION FOR EVOLUTION

We must do something we have never achieved in order to become something we have never been and feel what we have never known.

Consider the notion that the body, mind, and spirit are always changing, and that all you've ever been introduced to contributes to the recipe between how you are and who you're becoming.

For a few minutes, consider what you want to build or learn with your life. Then, for five minutes, perform breath consciousness meditation, experiencing the various thoughts and ideas that arise.

DAY 77

LIFE AS ART

All of us are artists, some are painters, musicians, performs, sculptors, but all of us live. We live our lives and imprint the universal memory with our beingness, colored by our attitudes and shaped by our choices.

DAY 78

TRANSMUTING ANGER

Today you will meditate on harmlessness, resisting anger and rage in all its forms. This isn't to become passive against genuine dangers but to transmute that energy into functionally power rather than self-destruction.

1. Get into a comfortable position, set a timer for at least five minutes, and close your eyes

2. Ask yourself, "What angers me?"

3. Observe your mind's automatic response.

4. Then ask, "How can I heal this?"

5. Observe your mind's response once more.

6. Continue to ask these two questions for the duration of the practice, giving just enough time in between for your mind to provide some kind of image or idea in response.

DAY 79

MINDFUL WEIGHT SHIFTING

Bring your awareness more deeply into the body with this practice of experiencing the subtle shifts in your weight with this exercise.

1. Stand with your feet shoulder width apart.

2. Keep both feet on the ground and slowly shift your weight to the right foot. Take three deep breaths and put your weight naturally pressing into the right foot.

3. Count the breaths, "one" on the inhale, "and" on the exhale, "two" on the inhale, "and" and on the exhale and so on.

4. Then slowly shift your weight to the left foot, taking three deep breaths on and out, counting them as before.

5. Alternate your weight between each foot for five minutes, moving slowly and mindfully.

DAY 80

PURE HARMONY

Though I am often in the depths of misery, there is still calmness, pure harmony and music inside me. I see paintings or drawings in the poorest cottages, in the dirtiest corners. And my mind is driven towards these things with an irresistible momentum. –

-Vincent Van Gogh

DAY 81

IN SYNC

Synchronicity is the recognition of meaningful coincidences. Have you ever noticed your birthday on the license plate of a car? Or met someone new who has the same name as your mother? From a positive psychology perspective, these meaningful coincidences can help us develop a sense that we are in the right place at the right time.

Look for synchronicities today, seek out meaningful coincidences and journal any that you may notice.

DAY 82

WATER BLESSING

Throughout the ages, world traditions have had a practice of blessing water before drinking or using it. It is said to sanctify the water and even change its molecular structure, enhancing its capacity for hydration and activating spiritual benefits. Make your glass of water a meditation.

1. Pour yourself a glass of water and take a seat.

2. Hold the glass in both hands and close your eyes for a moment.

3. Breathe in as you envision bright white light shining through every cell of the water silently saying “Bless this water.”

4. Breather out, silently saying, “Thank you, water”

5. Look at the water, and say out loud, “Bless you, water”

6. Then drink the water, after every sip, say out loud, “Thank you, water”

DAY 83

AFFIRMATION FOR POSITIVITY

"Every cause has its effect, and every effect has its cause. Today, I will move through life planting seeds of positivity and healing."

DAY 84

BREAKING MESMERISM

In the modern world we are inundated with distractions. Whether those distractions are advertisements, apps, or our own ambitions, we have to break the mesmerism and see things for what they really are. Observe the nature of the way your mind and feelings respond today. Journal about what you saw, how it made you feel, and if it caused you to think or believe something new, even in subtle ways.

Write objectively, honestly, and with non-judgement.

DAY 85

THE HOUSE OF SELF

"In zazen, leave your front door and your back door open. Let thoughts come and go, just don't serve them tea."

- Shunryu Suzuki -

DAY 86

MEDITATION ON SPIRITUAL AWAKENING

The lotus flower symbolizes spiritual awakening because it opens to awaken and receive the sunlight, and it closes to protect its fragile nature in the dark.

1. Get into a comfortable position, set your timer for at least five minutes, and close your eyes.

2. Envision a lotus flower glowing in golden light.

3. With every inhale, see the lotus blossom open, radiating light through every part of your body, mind, and spirit.

4. With every exhale, see the lotus closing and the body relaxing into the nourishment of the breath.

5. Continue until your timer goes off.

DAY 87

LOVE LETTERS TO THE UNIVERSE

Reflecting on your greatest personal challenges and the most significant problems humanity faces. In your journal or on a clean sheet of paper, you will write a letter to the universe about them featuring the following five components.

1. Begin by addressing the letter "Dear Universe…"

2. Declare the things you love about the world, offering gratitude for them.

3. Explain the problems you see and how you experience them.

4. Ask to be given signs and insight on how you can be a part of the solution.

5. Close by offering gratitude in advance for the answer and signing your name.

DAY 88

PRESENT MOMENT AWARENESS

Do not dwell in the past, do not dream of the future, concentrate the mind of the present moment. - Buddha, throughout your day, take an inventory of the thoughts occupying your mind. Are they focused on the past, present, or future? Practice bringing your attention back to the present moment,

DAY 89

THE MIRACLE OF FORGIVENESS

To forgive is to accept things as they are and to not judge or condemn the soul of the one you forgive. It is not necessary to reestablish a relationship with those you have forgiven, only that the release happens within your own heart.

DAY 90

SUNSHINE FOR LUNCH

Just as plants feed on the energy of sunlight, we absorb benefits from sunlight. Weather permitting for today's meditation, we will practice outdoors or near a window, in the sunlight.

Find a place to sit in the sunlight and set a timer for five minutes.

Rest your hands with your palms facing up as if they were solar panels able to absorb energy from the sun.

Close your eyes and bring your awareness to the breath.

Envision sunlight being absorbed through your skin, especially through your hands.

Observe the sensation of the warmth of the sun, the cool breeze, and everything else that comes up.

6. Visualize an energetic root system reaching from your body down into the ground

7. When the mind wanders, bring it back to the visualization and experience of the breath.

DAY 91

FIAT VERITAS

A Great teacher once said, *"The truth shall set you free"*. Meditate on this idea, contemplating its meaning for you as you silently repeat the mantra "Fiat Veritas," which means "let there be truth"

DAY 92

MEDITATION ON FLEXIBILITY

A flexible tree bends and sways with the wind, but a rigid tree breaks in a windstorm. Bringing a sense of playfulness and curiosity into our lives can allow for natural experience of flexibility and flow.

1. Get into a comfortable position and begin to meditate.

2. Breathing in and out, allow your body to relax deeper with every exhale.

3. Call to mind a memory when you were laughing and playing no matter how long ago it occurred.

4. Allow your inhales to bring that memory into the present moment.

5. Notice the sensations in the body and the thoughts that enter the mind.

6. Savor the joy and playfulness that arises. Bring it with you wherever you go today.

DAY 93

AFFIRMATION FOR EQUANIMITY

"There are ups and downs in life, but I will pause when agitated, breathe, and move on."

DAY 94

STARRING.....YOU!

You are the star of your own movie. Meditate to become more conscious of the character you live when nobody is watching.

1. Set a timer for at least five minutes and get into a comfortable position.

2. Take a few deep breaths and allow your body to relax.

3. Envision the room you are in, your actual environment, see it in your mind like a movie set.

4. Reflect on the post 24 hours, as if every single moment had been filmed.

5. Imagine the next 24 hours, all the places you'll go and things you'll do. What development will your character experience?

6. Take a few moments in meditation to reflect.

DAY 95

BREATHWORK

Clear away old energy and old ways of doing things by practicing conscious breathwork.

1. Breathe consciously one inhale into the belly, a second inhale into the chest, and then one full exhale.

2. Let the body become completely relaxed, signaling to the nervous system that old patterns can be cleared.

3. Silently repeat the phrase "Now is now" with every component of the breath. "Now" on the belly inhale, "Is" on the chest inhale, and "new" on the exhale.

Practice this breathwork exercise for five minutes. Then take three deep breaths in and out and set a mindful intention for yourself.

DAY 96

IKIGAI

In Japan, Ikigai is a powerful concept and that means "life purpose". Ikigai consists of the following four components.

1. That which you can be paid for.

2. That which you are skilled in.

3. That which you are passionate about.

4. That which the world needs.

People who can live in Ikigai are considered very enlightened.

Contemplate what it means for you and open your mind to new ways of being.

DAY 97

AFFIRMATION FOR INFINITE POSSIBILITIES

"I am in an infinite world with infinite possibilities"

DAY 98

PROCRASTINATION INSIGHT MEDITATION

If you ever feel that your heart just isn't invested in the tasks in front of you it could be that you feel disconnected from your purpose or that a task itself doesn't feel fulfilling.

1. Consider a task you may be putting off.

2. Ask yourself, "Why am I putting this off?"

3. Notice your mind's natural response.

4. Next, ask yourself, "Is this something I should be doing?"

5. Observe your mind's automatic answer.

6. Journal a few paragraphs about the task, your relationships to it, and what came up in meditation about why you may be putting it off.

DAY 99

VIBRATIONAL UNIVERSE

"Each celestial body, in fact each and every atom, produces a particular sound of its movement. Its rhythm or vibration. All these sounds and vibrations from a universal harmony in which each element, while having its own function and character, contributes to the whole."

- Pythagoras -

DAY 100

PSYCHIC COUNCIL

In this meditation, imagine a council of wise leaders and figures, always available to provide you with sage advice and guidance.

1. Consider the greatest challenge, concern, or goal you have.

2. Choose three historical, spiritual, or mythological figures to join your council.

3. Envision yourself in a comfortable room with your three council members.

4. Honestly and thoroughly present to them the different aspects of your challenge or goal.

5. Visualize them listening intently. Observe what your creative imagination presents each of them offering in response.

DAY 101

AFFIRMATION OF CONFIDENCE

"I have overcome so many things, and I am confident in my skills and abilities"

DAY 102

PIONEERING YOUR OWN PATH

There's no one quite like you, and your uniqueness is incredibly powerful! Today, set aside time to focus on "being "rather than "doing". Allowing yourself to be who you truly are doesn't negate the goals or desires to grow and improve but, rather, gives you the opportunity to consciously create yourself. You are the pioneer of your own life journey. Meditate using the mantra "I am the pioneer of my own life journey," releasing any expectations placed upon you and allowing yourself to just be.

DAY 103

MIND INVENTORY

In a journal or on a blank sheet of paper, write out a full page of whatever thoughts are coming to mind. Don't hold back. List everything you're thinking about, big and small, taking a full inventory of all that crosses your mind.

DAY 104

THE LITTLE THINGS

Contemplate something small in your life that you're grateful for.

Take a few breaths and really experience a sense of deep, sincere appreciation for it, no matter how small or insignificant it may seem.

It could be the warmth of sunlight on your skin, the softness of a pillow, or the sweetness of a fruit.

DAY 105

CONSCIOUS PLAYLIST

The music we listen to affects our mood in conscious and unconscious ways. Today, create a playlist that supports the kind of life you want to live. Be aware of the lyrics, tone and melody as you create your new conscious playlist.

DAY 106

EXPAND YOUR PERSPECTIVE

Find a comfortable position, allowing a wave of relaxation to pass through the body with every exhale. Become aware of any sounds or movement occurring in your immediate vicinity. And allow it to be part of the meditation with non-judgement.

Gradually expand your awareness and begin to envision the local area you live in, and then gradually see the region, observing all the many moving parts that come to mind. Allow your visualization to expand to include the nation, the continent, and then eventually the entire planet, seeing everything as part of one connected whole.

DAY 107

AFFIRMATION FOR OPTIMAL HEALTH

"My body is getting healthier and healthier every day, I am full of energy. My relationships are becoming more and more fulfilling every day. I am full of love. My mind is getting clearer and clearer every day. I am full of gratitude."

DAY 108

STRENGTH AND FLEXIBILITY

When we move through life with the strength of conviction, we maintain clear direction, and over time we achieve visible results.

When we navigate our challenges with grace and flexibility, we are less likely to be thrown off course. Strength and flexibility come together like a beautifully flowing but deliberate dance. Meditate on dancing through life in your stillness, call to mind different circumstances you are experiencing in your life now and see yourself graceful dancing through each one.

DAY 109

THEATER OF MIRRORS

"The entire universe is a great theatre of mirrors."

- Alice A. Bailey -

DAY 110

AFFIRMATION FOR DILIGENCE

"As I move through life, I do so with flexibility yet consistency. As I move through life, I do so with

playfulness yet reverence. As I move through life, I do so with power yet gentleness"

DAY 111

TONING MMM...

Take a few minutes to practice toning mantra meditation.

1. Take full and complete breaths
2. Let your exhales be long and complete, releasing a humming sound for the entire out breath. "Mmm…"
3. You may choose to experiment with different pitches, notes, or tones with each exhale "Mmm".
4. Focus your attention on the experience of the vibration throughout your body.

DAY 112

MINDFUL DREAM INTERPRETATION

The dreams and visions we have when we sleep are gateways of profound insight into our unconscious minds. Recall a dream you recently had, not judging any aspect of to, and write it down.

1. Setting: Where were you in the dream?
2. Characters: who or what else was there?
3. Events: What was happening?
4. Tone: How did you feel?

Reflect on this dream and consider the following interpretations.

1. Setting: This symbolizes the stage of life you are in.
2. Characters: These symbolize various aspects of yourself.
3. Events: These symbolize dynamics at play in your life
4. Tone: This symbolizes what your psyche is processing.

DAY 113

BLOSSOM

Meditate and envision every part of your body blooming with flowers on every exhale, watching them close into buds on every inhale.

DAY 114

AFFIRMATION FOR LIFE MASTERY

"There are no failures, only lessons, and I love to learn. There are no problems, only lessons, and I love to learn. There are no challenges, only lessons, and I love to learn."

DAY 115

LOVE MAKES PERFECT

Even with all your character defects, quirks, and foibles, you are perfectly lovable, loved, and worthy of love.

DAY 116

BODY BALANCER

Standing comfortably, practice this variation of a mindful body scan.

1. Allow your arms to rest comfortably at your side and close your eyes.

2. Bring your awareness throughout the right side of your body.

3. Softly tighten at the muscles on your right your calf, thigh, chest, arm, etc.

4. Release the muscles on your right side, and then softly tighten the muscles on your left side.

5. Make sure to take a few comfortable deep breaths as you do this.

6. Alternate between the right side and the left side three times, then gently tighten and release the muscles on both sides of the body

7. Take three deep breaths, relaxing every part of the body.

DAY 117

RISE AND SHINE

Whether you meditate first thing in the morning at midday, in the afternoon, or just before bed, give yourself a minute to "rise and shine". Take a few moments to meditate silently. When you finish, stand up and stretch your arms, and smile nice and big. Envision light shining from all directions around you, like sunlight.

DAY 118

THIS IS EXACTLY WHAT I WANT TO BE DOING

Throughout your day today, become very present with whatever task is at hand. Bring your attention to the different aspects of what you are doing, whether it is a task you consider a chore or a joy, treat it the same. Silently repeat the mantra "This is exactly what I want to be doing" to help keep you in the moment. Notice how it changes the experience.

DAY 119

MINDFUL SELF-CARE

When we don't practice adequate self-care, we don't set ourselves up to feel and act like our true selves. A very well-known concept in meditation is that "meditation helps you become more and more you". A quote commonly attributed to David Lynch but that is actually a more universal concept. Self-care can mean a lot of different things to different people. Reflect on your own personal circumstances and remind yourself that you can only contribute as well as you're actually feeling. What does mindful self-care mean for you? What can you do to take better care of yourself so you can be more "you" in your life?

DAY 120

FIAT LUX

Light is symbolic for understanding, recognition, realization, and goodness. In the dark, we are unable to see, but when there is light, we can see clearly. Meditate using the mantra "Fiat Lux", which means "Let there be light," invoking clarity, wisdom, and enlightenment in the deepest darkest corners of your mind

DAY 121

INITIATION

Initiation means to begin something new with a new level of understanding. Allow today, to be a day of initiation. Meditate on how far you've come in life, the challenges you've triumphantly overcome, and the things you've learned. Move forward today with a sense of confidence and humanity. Every day is an initiation into our future.

DAY 122

MINDFUL HYDRATION

Fit a glass of water and have a seat with it. Imagine the taste and sensation in your mouth before you have your first sip. Take a small drink and notice the temperature and taste of the water. Observe the subtle sensations throughout the mouth and throat. Practice drinking slowly and mindfully, as if this glass of water were a fine wine, focusing directly on the experience of it. Notice when the mind wanders or the attention gets distracted, take a deep breath, and come back to the water.

DAY 123

INTENTION SETTING

Set a meaningful intention for yourself in meditation today. As we "in-tend", we are "invoking tendencies," meaning that we are calling forth new qualities of being from within ourselves.

Ask yourself.

1. What do I want to achieve?
2. What are some qualities that others who have successfully achieved this possess?
3. What are the thoughts that may occur in the mind of one who achieves this?

DAY 124

AFFIRMATION FOR PRESENT MOMENT AWARENESS

"I am right here, right now. This moment is all there truly is. All my power exists in the present moment."

DAY 125

CASTING THE BURDEN

We can often feel burdened by a seemingly insurmountable goal or challenge that we face. Direct your attention to the successful achievement and fulfilment of your goal or to the complete and total resolution of the challenge, imagining the possibility of total success and complete peace. Cast the energetic burden of this challenge or goal aside for now, planting the seed of your vision deeply in your mind in meditation.

DAY 126

SILENCE AND DARKNESS

No durable things are built on violent passion. Nature grows her plants in silence and in darkness, and only when they have become strong do they put their heads above the ground. -Anne Besant

DAY 127

ALCHEMY

Alchemy was said to be the ancient practice of turning less-desirable metals into gold. In psychological alchemy, we liberate ourselves from our own reactive nature, transmuting the less desirable automatic reactions into the gold of wise responsiveness.

1. Reflect on an instance when you may have made impetuous or rash decisions.

2. Breathe through any residual challenging feelings that may come up, allowing your body to relax.

3. Let go of any frustration or negativity associated with the experience, accepting it as a lesson and opportunity to grow.

4. Imagine the circumstances of your reactivity and begin to envision yourself navigating similar situations with wisdom and grace.

DAY 128

GRATITUDE

Consider the technology and tools that assist you in getting through the day. Take a few deep breaths and express gratitude for the utility of something you normally take for granted.

DAY 129

MOMENT OF METTA

Take five minutes to send lovingkindness to people who are less fortunate than you all over the world.

DAY 130

AFFIRMATION TO BE FREE OF THE NEED FOR APPROVAL

"I do not need others' approval for contentment. I am deserving of contentment right now, and I do not need others' approval for peace. I am deserving of peace right here and now, I do not need others' approval for joy. I am deserving of joy right here and now"

DAY 131

FAILURE SCHMAILURE

Take the sting out of failure through a lighthearted reflection.

1. Have a seat and rest your hands open in your lap.

2. Bring awareness to your breath.

3. Fix a smile on your face and breathe into it, letting a sense of levity fill your body.

4. Ask yourself, "What are some of my biggest failures?"

5. Listen to your mind's response feel free to laugh at it!

6. Ask yourself, "What have I learned?"

7. Listen to your mind's response and visualize yourself applying that which you have learned.

8. Ask yourself, "How can I apply this now?"

DAY 132

THE POWER OF HONESTY

We learn and grow through mistakes. The challenge comes when our fears or insecurities prevent us from being honest with ourselves and others about our mistakes. Without an outlet for honesty, shame, and guilt can take hold and lead to psychological or emotional unwellness. Let go of the weight of perfectionism today.

Be honest with a trusted friend today about some of your imperfections, challenges, or mistakes.

DAY 133

ASK FOR GUIDANCE

1. Relax into a comfortable position and begin to meditate.

2. Ask yourself, “What is it that I really want?”

3. Listen without judgement to the mind’s answer.

4. Ask yourself, “What is it that will bring me real fulfilment?”

5. Observe the mind and note what you discover.

DAY 134

COUNTERACTING THE STRESS RESPONSE

Practice present moment awareness. Allow your body to decompress and soften into the present moment, taking deep, full inhales, and deep, complete exhales. This will trigger a relaxation response in the body, diluting stress hormones and making your stressors more manageable.

DAY 135

MEDITATION ON JOY

Make a list of five things that bring you joy. Then meditate on the:

1. Take a few deep breaths and settle into a comfortable position.
2. Bring the first item in your joy list to mind.
3. Breathe into it. Feel and embody the joy it brings.
4. Go through each item on your list filling your heart and mind with joy.
5. When you're finished, share that joy with others today through kindness and generosity.

DAY 136

AFFIRMATION FOR SELF-CREATION

"I create who I become. My past is not a prophecy of my future. I love who I am becoming"

DAY 137

PARADE OF THOUGHTS

The mind is always thinking. When it's racing, settle into a comfortable position and close your eyes. Observe the thoughts as they arise in the mind as if they were parade floats, coming and going. Continue to breathe in and out, never holding the breath.

DAY 138

MINDFUL COORDINATION

1. Set a timer for about five minutes, sit comfortably and let your body relax.

2. Clench your left fist tightly and breathe in.

3. Breathe out as you release your left fist.

4. Clench your right fist tightly and breathe in.

5. Breathe out as you release your right fist.

6. Continue to coordinate your breath with alternating right and left fists, breathing in as you tightly clench one fist at a time and releasing all tension on every exhale.

7. When your timer goes off, shake your hands out and take a few deep breaths.

DAY 139

EMOTIONAL HYGIENE

Practice emotional hygiene today by cleansing yourself of uncomfortable emotions prior to interacting with others. Here are some ways you can cleanse yourself of uncomfortable emotions.

1. Meditate
2. Shut it out or fence it off
3. Take a nap
4. Take a shower
5. Journal

DAY 140

AFFIRMATION OF MINDFULNESS

"How you do anything is how you do everything so I choose to do things well. How you do anything is how you everything, so I choose to do things intentionally. How you do anything is how you do everything so I choose to do things mindfully."

DAY 141

FOR THE BENEFIT OF ALL BEINGS

1. Set a timer for at least five minutes and sit comfortably.

2. Say silently to yourself, *"May I be happy, harmless, safe from harm, helpful, and healthy for the benefit of all beings."*

3. Visualize your friends and family, saying silently, *"May you be happy, harmless, safe from harm, helpful, and healthy for the benefit of all things."*

4. Call to mind coworkers, neighbors, and those with whom you have difficulty, silently saying, *"May you be happy, harmless, safe from harm, helpful, and healthy for the benefit of all things."*

DAY 142

THERMAL EXERCISE IN THE SHOWER

Exposing your body to temperatures outside the normal comfort zone is a great way to practice non-attachment and is proven to have incredible health benefits for boosting the immune system, managing depression, and much more.

1. Take a shower and finish cleaning your body in your normal routine.

2. Increase the temperature slightly above what you would normally consider comfortable.

3. Take a few deep breaths in the hot water, allowing the body to relax.

4. Then decrease the temperature slightly below what you would normally consider comfortable.

5. Take a few deep breaths on the cold water, allowing the body to relax once more before you finish your shower.

DAY 143

COUNTING THE BREATH

Sit comfortably, set a timer for at least five minutes, close your eyes, and breathe normally. Silently count your breaths.

Exhale, “one…”

Inhale, “and….”

Exhale, “two…”

Inhale, “and….”

Continue until you reach 10 and then start again at one.

DAY 144

AFFIRMATION FOR ENJOYING THE PROCESS

“Even though some things may seem uncertain, I can enjoy the process. Even though some things may seem uncomfortable, I can enjoy the process. Even though some things may seem unusual, I can enjoy the process”

DAY 145

INNER REFLECTION

“There is only one life yet infinite points of view”

1. Sit in a comfortable position, set your timer for at least five minutes and begin to meditate.

2. Visualize the first person who comes to mind sitting across from you.
3. Imagine that you are looking comfortably into their eyes.
4. Breathe in and out, holding the breath.
5. Imagine that as you look into their eyes you are looking into a mirror.
6. Let your whole body be very relaxed.
7. As you inhale, see them inhaling.
8. As you exhale, see them exhaling.
9. After a few breaths, raise your left hand, and see them raise theirs simultaneously.
10. Wave your left hand watching them mirror you.
11. Place your hand down, and do the same exercise with your right hand.
12. Observe the thoughts that arise, but keep the awareness focused on the visualization until your timer goes off.

DAY 146

STARDUST

"....the cosmos is also within us. We're made of star stuff. We are a way for the cosmos to know itself."

- Carl Sagan -

Take a look at the stars in a clear night sky. Consider each star to be our living ancient ancestors, capable of seeing and hearing you. Consider the possibility and reality that our bodies are made up of many different natural components that we do not fully comprehend.

DAY 147

UNDERSTANDING OURSELVES

"Everything that irritates us about others can lead us to an understanding of ourselves."

- Carl Jung -

DAY 148

DETACH FROM OUTCOMES

It is good to have driven and enthusiasm to achieve certain goals, and it is also good to work hard toward that end. But having an attachment to a specific outcome can lead to suffering. Practice detaching from certain outcomes, even though it may seem contrary to your commitment to goals and visions. There are many ways we can enjoy a fulfilling life. Enjoy the process and learn from every experience.

DAY 149

ALTERNATE NOSTRIL BREATHING

1. Sit upright on a cushion or in a chair and let your shoulders relax.

2. Let your left hand rest in your lap, keeping your eyes and mouth closed.

3. Exhale, emptying your lungs completely.

4. With your right thumb, close your right nostril.

5. Inhale through your left nostril

6. With your right index finger, close your left nostril.

7. Open your right nostril and exhale completely. Then inhale completely.

8. Close your right nostril and open your left nostril, inhaling and exhaling.

9. Continue for five minutes, staying focused on the present moment.

DAY 150

AFFIRMATION FOR COMPASSION

"I have compassion for myself and others. My heart is full to overflowing with compassion. In the center of my heart is an infinite portal of compassion."

DAY 151

PATIENCE

As you practice the virtue of patience, you develop a subtle refinement in your personality. When we rush things, we often find ourselves with something of lesser value. When we are patient, we give room for higher quality to manifest. Cultivate patience in this stillness meditation.

1. Set your timer for five to 30 minutes.

2. Allow every inhale to bring fulfilment, as if you are drinking a cool glass of water on a hot summer day.

3. Allow every exhale to bring relief, as if you are completing a challenging exercise.

4. Enjoying every breath until your timer goes off.

DAY 152

CARPE DIEM

Our daily schedules and immediate tasks can become mundane and burn us out or deflate our enthusiasm for life. Today, meditate using the mantra "Carpe Diem", which means "seize the day"

DAY 153

RIGHT PLACE AND TIME

Consider that you are already exactly where you need to be for your greatest learning and joy.

Imagine that everything is happening exactly as it should and that you are in the right place at the right time, right here and now.

DAY 154

FACIAL MASSAGE

Sit or stand comfortably and let all the muscles in your body relax.

Using the first and second fingers of both hands, gently massage your temples, your cheekbones, your jaw, around your eyes, your forehead, your eyebrows, and your ears. Take deep breaths before, after, and during your massage.

DAY 155

SELF-ACCEPTANCE

Practice accepting yourself exactly as you are now. Throughout your day today, treat yourself as you would a good friend.

DAY 156

AFFIRMATION FOR OVERCOMING

"Although I may not know everything, I know enough to know things work out. Although I may not see exactly how things will work out, I know everything is okay. Although everything may not seem okay, I know this is part of the process."

DAY 157

PRESENT MOMENT LISTENING

Close your eyes, relax into a comfortable position, and settle in. Become aware of all the subtle sounds happening all around you.

Listen with no attachment to any particular sound, as if your ears were recording the audio of the present moment.

DAY 158

THANK YOU NOTES

There is so much to be thankful for. Take some time today to consider all the wonderful people in your life and the big (or small) ways they make the world a better place.

1. Make a list of 10 friends, family members, or acquaintances.

2. Write them each a short but thoughtful thank you note-- the more specific, the better. You can text, email or handwrite the note.

3. Make sure they receive it today.

DAY 159

HEARTFULNESS MEDITATION

One definition of mindfulness is to “fill every aspect of the present moment with the awareness of your mind” Based on that definition, heartfulness can be defined as “to fill every aspect of the present moment with heart” Practice a heartfulness meditation today.

1. Bring your awareness to your heart center and observe the beating of your heart from the inside.

2. Imagine the pulse of your heartbeat radiating out in all directions around you, filling your environment with your deepest sincerity, compassion, and love.

3. When the mind wanders, bring your focus back to that sense of sincerity, compassion, and love placed directly on the heartbeat.

DAY 160

TO LOVE AND TO BE LOVED

To love and to be loved, one must do good to others. The inevitable condition whereby to become blessed is to bless others. -Mary Baker Eddy

DAY 161

BODY GRATITUDE

Contemplate your body and all the many powerful, wonderful functions it serves. Take a few breaths of deep, true gratitude for the body and its inability to heal and grow all on its own. Silently repeat the words "thank you, thank you, thank you…." as you exhale to help you cultivate and embody this sense of gratitude.

DAY 162

AFFIRMATION FOR PREPAREDNESS

"I could never be prepared for everything so I choose to prepared for anything"

DAY 163

CHANGE OF HEART

A change of heart is the opportunity to feel differently about something by realizing an attachment or a judgement. It never means to condone or justify harmful behavior but to liberate ourselves from the unconscious mental baggage of a limiting belief.

1. Get into a comfortable position, set a time for at least five minutes, and begin to meditate.

2. Relax your body and bring your awareness into your heart center.

3. Observe your mind and the different thoughts and ideas that arise.

4. As thoughts arise, whether they are loving, fearful, joyful, or worried, repeat the phrase *"A change of heart is possible. I am willing to love even more."*

5. When your timer goes off, place both hands over your heart and say out loud, *"A change*

of heart is possible. I am willing to love even more."

DAY 164

INFLUENCE

Practice mindful awareness of how everything affects you. Notice headlines and status updates and how they can trigger emotions or ac as distractions.

DAY 165

MEDITATION TO RELEASE TENSION

One of the best visual symbols for our awareness is light. We can envision a spotlight on something when we are focused on it, and we can envision the glow of a candle flame when we have an open awareness in the moment.

1. Take a few moments to meditate, using the "spotlight" of your awareness to scan through the body, finding any areas of tightness or tension.

2. When you find them, send an exhale of relaxation directly into the tension.

Gradually releasing all the tension in your body, notice the warm glow of your awareness shining in all directions around you.

DAY 166

ANYTIME ENERGIZER

Yawn and stretch for 30 seconds and clap your hands three times for a quick mindful energizer.

DAY 167

QUICK LUNG STRETCH

Alternate breathing into the belly and the back using the following directions.

1. Set a timer for at least five minutes, sit comfortably, and close your eyes.
2. Take a deep breath into the belly, stretching the lungs just a bit at the top of the inhale.
3. Hold for three… two….. One…..
4. Empty the lungs entirely on the exhale, pushing all the air out.

5. Hold for three… two….. One…..

6. Take a deep breath into your back, filling the lungs entirely.

7. Hold for three… two….. One…..

8. Breathe out, emptying the lungs.

9. Hold for three… two….. One…..

10. Continue until your timer goes off.

DAY 168

AFFIRMATION FOR HEALING AND GROWTH

"My body heals naturally, as do my heart and mind. My body adapts naturally, as do my heart and mind. My body evolves naturally, as do my heart and mind."

DAY 169

DISENGAGE

As you practice mindfulness meditation, you gradually begin to realize how easy it is to stop taking your thoughts so seriously many of them are not even true! This naturally begins to help you disengage from the very common concern of what others are thinking about you, many of their thoughts are untrue as well.

Meditate for five or more minutes today with special emphasis on not taking your thoughts so seriously.

DAY 170

AD LUCEM

Enlightenment is the total realization of truth in the present moment, free from any illusions, attachments, or distortions. Silently repeat the mantra “Ad Lucem” which means “on to enlightenment”.

DAY 171

LOVESTORM

Take a few minutes to meditate and send metta loving kindness to every person you will see and places where you will find yourself today.

1. Have a seat and rest your open hands in your lap.

2. Bring your awareness to your breath.

3. Fill your heart, body, and mind with compassion and acceptance for yourself.

4. Once you feel the love, begin to notice who comes to mind, offering everyone and everything the same compassion and acceptance as received.

5. Deliberately bring to mind anyone you may see today, showering them with lovingkindness, especially anyone with whom you may have difficulty.

6. Visualize any places you may be going today and mentally fill the rooms and buildings with lovingkindness.

DAY 172

AFFIRMATION FOR SELF-CONTROL

"I alone am in control over my body and my mind. When I find myself overcome or distracted, it is only my own free agency that can override the experience and bring me back to center."

DAY 173

TONING EEE….

Take a few minutes to practice toning mantra meditation, placing the awareness on the vibrational sensations throughout the body.

1. Get into a comfortable position, set a time for at least 5 minutes, and close your eyes

2. Breathe into the top, bottom, left, right, front and back sides of the lungs.

3. Let your exhales be ling and complete, releasing a toning sound for the entire out breath, "eee…

4. Keep the tone and note consistent throughout the exhale, but feel free to

experiment with different tones and notes on each exhale.

DAY 174

GREATNESS

"......be not afraid of greatness. Some are born great, some achieve greatness, and some have greatness thrust upon 'em."

- William Shakespeare -

DAY 175

MEDITATION OF HEALING LIGHT

1. Sit cross-legged or upright in a chair.

2. Relax every muscle in the body with every exhale.

3. Observe your thoughts and the sounds, smells, and feelings you're experiencing now.

4. Visualize a spark of empowering light behind your eyes in the very center of your brain.

5. Envision this light growing brighter and filling the entire head and neck, improving your brain.

6. Visualize this light expanding and filling every part of the spine and nervous system, healing and supercharging your physical body.

7. Imagine each and every organ and gland, tissue, muscle, bone and fluid in your body glowing with this same light.

8. Let it nourish and relax you, as if this light is providing exactly what every part of the body needs.

9. Relax a little bit deeper and shine a little bit brighter with every exhale.

DAY 176

ALL IS CONNECTED

1. Stand comfortably in a quiet place for a standing meditation.

2. Close your eyes and mentally scan the space in all directions around you.

3. Hold an open awareness of all the sensory input coming from all directions.

4. Imagine that your awareness is an extension of your body and that your body does not end on the surface of your skin.

5. Envision that everything you can hear or sense in all directions around you is an extension of your body.

6. Contemplate the connectedness of all things, picturing the entire plant as a body and every living thing as a cell in the body.

DAY 177

AFFIRMATION FOR ENCOURAGEMENT

"My journey of healing and growth, and evolution is a path of courage and strength. My journey of healing, growth, and evolution affects not only me

but all those around me. My journey of healing, growth, and evolution affects not only me but all future generations"

DAY 178

BALANCED SITTING

1. Sit down with your back erect and both feet flat on the floor.

2. Rest both hands flat down on your thighs.

3. On your inhales, allow your spine to elongate upward slightly toward the ceiling, as if it were attached to a string being pulled up.

4. On your exhales, send a wave of decompression through all the muscles in the body.

5. Allow the vertebrae in the spine to rest one by one on top of one another.

6. Breathe comfortably and find your balance.

DAY 179

THE POWER OF THE WORD

Throughout your day today, become extra cognizant of the words you speak. Imagine that every word you speak takes literal form on some level. Words can and do have unconscious influence in our minds and the minds of all those who hear them. Choose your words wisely.

DAY 180

MIRROR VISUALIZATION

1. Close your eyes and set a timer for at least five minutes.

2. Visualize yourself sitting in the center of a beautiful white room, once you can "feel" is a sacred place in a higher dimension, just for your own personal meditation.

3. Visualize mirrors with beautiful golden frames.

4. See one mirror on the left wall and one on the right wall, facing each other.

5. Visualize a mirror on the wall in front of you and behind you as well as on the ceiling above you and the floor beneath you,

6. Notice any images that may arise in your mind as you challenge yourself to open your mind and hold the visualization of all six mirrors.

DAY 181

COUNTING MEDITATION AND MENTAL NOTING

Practice thought awareness, develop concentration, and increase mental control with today's meditation.

1. Get comfortable, allowing the body to relax and settle in, and begin to meditate.

2. Count from one to 10, and note the different thoughts that arise, no matter how small.

3. When a thought comes up, observe it and identify it. "This is a thought about work" or "This is a thought about my family."

4. After you identify the thought, go back to counting, starting at one.

5. If you reach 10 without a thought arising, make sure you are noticing even your subtle thoughts and continue back at one.

DAY 182

AFFIRMATION AND CLEANSING

"As I breathe in, new life fills every cell of my being. As I breathe out, I release old patterns of living as I breathe in, new possibilities fill every thought in my mind. As I breathe out, I release old patterns of thinking. As I breathe in, new love fills every beat of my heart. As I breathe out, I release old patterns of feeling."

DAY 183

MOUNTAINTOP VISUALIZATION MEDITATION

For today's meditation, you may sit up or lie down. Meditate for at least five minutes and allow your body to be as relaxed as possible.

1. With every exhale, send a wave of relaxation throughout the body.

2. Visualize yourself sitting at the top of a peaceful mountain.

3. Observe the view as far as you can see, notice the sky, plants, animals, and everything else you can see.

4. Cultivate a sense of serenity and peace, stimulating a relaxing meditation in nature.

5. Breathe in and out, full but gentle breaths, never holding the breath.

6. Allow different thoughts to arise and pass through your mind, always bringing your awareness back to the visualization.

DAY 184

TENDON AND MUSCLE OBSERVATION MEDITATION

Bring yourself into a comfortable sitting position. Let your hands rest pams down on your thighs. Take a few deep breaths and relax your entire body.

Once you have settled in and become still, begin the following exercise.

1. Become aware of the stillness in your body.
2. Inhale and gently lift both your pinkies up off your thighs, keeping every other part of your body relaxed.
3. Notice the sensation of the tendons, nerves, and muscles that lift these fingers up.
4. Gently exhale, lowering the pinky fingers.
5. Continue with each set of fingers two more times, pairing the inhale with the lift and the exhale with the lower.
6. Allow the body to be relaxed, becoming aware of the subtle movements with each action.

DAY 185

MINDFUL EATING VARIATION

Eat something new and make this meal your meditation.

1. Take a few deep breaths before your first bite.

2. Cultivate a sense of appreciation for what you are about to eat.

3. Notice the smell and appearance of the food, describing it without using judgmental terms like good or bad.

4. Take a small bite. Move the food around in your mouth and experience the flavor and texture. Chew and swallow slowly, present with the entire process.

5. Observe the food internally as you swallow it, feeling it move into your stomach.

6. Notice the way the food makes you feel as you eat it and afterward.

DAY 186

AFFIRMATION FOR MIRACLES

"I am open to seeing things differently. I am willing to see things differently. I am determined to see things differently."

DAY 187

LETTING GO OF UNWANTED BEHAVIORS

For this meditation, we will address any unwanted behaviors that don't serve our well-being and open ourselves up to another way of living.

1. Find a comfortable position. Allow your exhales to send a wave of relaxation throughout the nervous system and every muscle, disengaging from the past.

2. Allow every inhale to expand the lungs in all directions, experiencing a recalibration with every breath.

3. Maintaining relaxed stillness, begin to communicate with every aspect of yourself, saying. "Thank you for everything, I need your help now. Please let go entirely of the unwanted behavior of ____________. Please eliminate dysfunctional thoughts that support that behavior. Replace them with

healthy thoughts. Please eliminate desires that support that behavior

4. Replace them with healthy desires. Thank you."

5. Observe what comes up in your mind, breathing through it.

6. When your meditation ends, stretch your body in whatever way is comfortable.

DAY 188

FROM WITHIN OUTWARD

"The Universe is worked and guided from within outwards."

- Helena Petrovna Blavetsky -

DAY 189

ABANDON OUR VIEWS

In order to grow and transform, we have to abandon the views that have kept us stuck in old ways of operating. Take out a clean sheet of paper and write a letter to yourself about the views that are preventing you from overcoming your greatest challenges. Be as loving and encouraging as possible.

DAY 190

AFFIRMATION FOR HONESTY

"There are enough illusions, so I will communicate only the truth. There are enough deceptions, so I will offer only integrity, There are enough lies, so I will offer only honesty."

DAY 191

FORGIVING KINDNESS MEDITATION

Practice a variation on a traditional lovingkindness meditation.

1. Get into a comfortable position and set your timer for five or more minutes.

2. Sit tall and silently say to yourself, "I forgive myself for any shortcomings, perceived or real. I deserve total love and acceptance. May I be healed."

3. Bring to mind close loved ones and silently say to them, "I forgive you for any

shortcomings, perceived or real. You deserve total love and acceptance. May you be healed."

4. Now envision your friends and neighbors, coworkers, colleagues, and acquaintances, silently telling them the same message.

5. Next, bring it to mind those with whom you have difficulty, offering them the same forgiveness.

6. Finally, send that same message to all the world. Envision people from all walks of life, all plants and animals, and the earth itself.

DAY 192

CONFIDENCE AND HUMILITY WRITING EXERCISE

Healthy confidence is humble and strong, while unhealthy confidence is arrogant and abrasive. For this writing exercise, ask yourself, *"How can I rewrite the current story of my life so that I am a triumphant overcomer while still expressing enlightened humility?"*

DAY 193

ALL IS WELL

Establish a sense that "all is well" with this practice of conscious breathwork.

1. Set a timer for five minutes and get into a comfortable position.

2. Breather consciously, one inhale into the belly, a second inhale into the chest, and then a full exhale.

3. Let the body become completely relaxed, signaling to the nervous system that old patterns can be cleared.

4. Silently repeat the phrase, "All is well" with every component of the breath, "all" on the belly inhale, "is "on the chest inhale, and "well "on the exhale.

When the timer goes off, take three deep breaths and set an intention for yourself.

DAY 194

AFFIRMATION FOR ENLIGHTENMENT

"I am not afraid of the truth, and so I open my eyes to see it. I am not afraid of the truth, and so I open my mind to understand it. I am not afraid of the truth, and so I open my heart to feel it."

DAY 195

VESSEL FOR LOVE BODY SCAN

Send the message to your body that you love and accept it, exactly as it is, recognizing that it is always changing and growing. Embrace the idea that this body exists to be a vessel for giving and receiving love.

1. Lie down comfortably flat on your back.

2. Close your eyes and take a few deep breaths.

3. Scan your awareness to every part of your body, beginning with your head and moving your way all the way down to your feet.

4. Silently say, "I love and accept you completely."

5. Visualize a portal of infinite love, deep in the center of every cell that makes up your body.

6. Allow that love to fill every part of the body and radiate in all directions around you.

DAY 196

THE TEMPTING MOMENT

Remember not only to say the right thing in the right place, but far more difficult still to leave unsaid the wrong thing at the tempting moment. - Benjamin Franklin

DAY 197

ACCEPTANCE IN ALL DIRECTIONS

Suffering and frustration come from unmet desires and unrealized expectations. Cultivate acceptance and non-attachment to outcome with this simple meditation.

1. Sit upright, get into a comfortable position, and settle in.

2. While keeping your body motionless, mentally scan the space to your left, accepting everything exactly as it is, not trying to change one single thing. Take five deep breaths with your attention fixed on your left.

3. Then scan your awareness to your right, accepting everything exactly as it is, and taking five deep breaths focusing on your right.

4. Next, direct your attention to the space behind you, accepting everything exactly as it is and taking five deep breaths in and out.

5. Bring your awareness to the space in front of you, taking five deep breaths and accepting everything exactly as it is.

6. Tune your awareness to the space below you, breathing deeply for five breaths in

deep acceptance of things as they are below you.

7. Finally, mentally scan the space above you, observing and accepting things exactly as they are. Take five deep breaths.

DAY 198

AFFIRMATION FOR SELF CONTROL

"I am aware of my thoughts and I am the gatekeeper of those I allow, I am aware of my words, and I am the gatekeeper of those I speak, I am aware of my impulses and I am the gatekeeper of those that manifest into action."

DAY 199

YOU ARE HERE

Develop yourself awareness by expanding it beyond your immediate environment in this meditation.

1. Set a timer for at least five minutes for your meditation, close your eyes, and bring the awareness into the breath.

2. Visualize yourself in your current environment, see a 360-Degree view in all directions around you.

3. Welcome the sensations in your body, your emotions, and anything else that presents itself to you.

4. Visualize the immediate surroundings, the building and neighborhood you are in.

5. Taking your time, breathing in and out, begin to visualize the city, region, and nation you are currently in.

6. Visualize the planet you are on, including the rotation and orbit you're currently in.

7. Visualize the planet in orbit around the sun, with all other planets.

8. Visualize the solar system in orbit around the galactic center of our galaxy.

9. See beyond our galaxy until you see many other galaxies throughout the cosmos.

DAY 200

TAKING INTEREST

Today, practice listening more than you speak. As you move throughout your day, ask more questions. Take more of an interest in another person's perspective or experience. Be as attentive and receptive as possible while they are giving their responses.

DAY 201

DELIBERATE CREATION

In this meditation, visualize a certain outcome, a small goal or a big dream, and live backward from it.

1. Select one goal or intention to work with.

2. Get into a comfortable position and let the body relax.

3. Begin by visualizing your intention or goal as clearly as possible.

4. In your mind's eye, begin to "rewind time" from that successfully achieved goal.

5. Observe the different actions, decisions, and experiences that lead up to that goal.

6. Ask yourself, "What practical actions can I take to increase the chances of this becoming a reality?"

DAY 202

OMNE REMEDIUM

A relaxed body strengthens and improves faster. A calm mind does as well. Relax your body and mind by meditating for at least five minutes and silently repeating the mantra *"Omne Remedium,"* which translates to "every remedy" or "cure-all." Return to the mantra whenever your mind wanders. With each exhale, visualize every part of your body, heart, and mind receiving the exact treatment required.

DAY 203

THERE IS HAPPINESS

Emotions can be extremely powerful. If we say, “I am sad” this mentally acts as an affirmation, creating more of the emotion we are experiencing.

One way we can allow emotions to come and go more easily is by “noting” them rather than identifying with them. Meditate today and note the emotions you experience.

Instead of saying, “I am sad,” say, “There is sadness” Even practice this with positive emotions, for example, if you are happy, say “There is happiness”.

DAY 204

TAKE WHAT COMES

“This is the precept by which I have lived. Prepare for the worst, expect the best, and take what comes.”

- Hannah Arendt -

DAY 205

MINDFUL WINK COORDINATION

1. Set a timer for about five minutes.

2. Sit comfortably and let your body relax, resting with your eyes again.

3. Close your left eye, keeping your right eye open and breathe in.

4. Breathe out as you open your left eye.

5. Close your right eye and breathe in.

6. Breathe out as you open your right eye.

7. Continue to coordinate your breath with alternating blinks, breathing in with one closed eye at a time and disengaging from all tension on every exhale.

8. When your timer goes off, blink your eyes open and closed and take a few deep breaths.

DAY 206

AFFIRMATION FOR GENUINE AMENDS

"I open myself up to releasing the discomfort and pain of the rifts that have occurred in my

relationships with myself and others. I intend to integrate the lesson and move forward with wisdom and forgiveness. I am open to seeing things differently."

DAY 207

TRUE VIRTUE INSIGHT MEDITATION

You have an inherent understanding of what it means to be virtuous. The chaos and mixed messages of the world can leave us feeling confused and thinking that what's not good for us is what we want. Practice this insight meditation to recalibrate your higher nature and true virtue.

1. Take a free minute to meditate and set a timer for at least five minutes.

2. Ask yourself, "What does it mean for me to be virtuous?"

3. Notice your mind's natural response. Breathe and take your time.

4. Ask again, "What does it mean for me to be virtuous?"

5. Relax the body as you continue to ask the same question, observing the many ways your mind will respond.

DAY 208

SURF THE WAVES

The places we go, things we do, and experiences we have can be linked to the waves of the ocean. Sometimes there are rough seas, and other times there are calm waters. A masterful surfer can surf these waves and enjoy the exhilarating sensation in the process.

Stubbornness has no place out on the open ocean, a skilled sailor submits to what is there, navigating the waves with grace and precision. Throughout your day, surf through whatever occurs.

Navigate your challenges with the wisdom and skill of a champion surfer or an experienced sailor

DAY 209

MINDFUL BREATHING

Meditate for at least five minutes today.

1. With your eyes closed, breathe in through the nose and out through the mouth.

2. Slowly and gradually fill your lungs as you inhale.

3. Slowly and gradually empty your lungs as you exhale.

4. Mentally observe all the different sensations in your body and any sensory input from your surroundings.

5. Constantly breathe in and out, slowly and gradually, never holding the breath.

DAY 210

AFFIRMATION FOR DETERMINATION

"Challenges arise, but they do not slow me down. Celebrations arise but I continue on. More to come, more to come, more to come."

DAY 211

A NOVEL IDEA

Today's, meditation is a reflection on your life as if it were a bestselling novel. Reflect on your character, setting and experiences. Let this be fun, light and easy!

1. Get comfortable, set a time for at least five minutes, and begin to meditate.

2. Allow the body to become relaxed.

3. Begin to mentally describe yourself in the third person, rather than saying, "I am ___" say, "They are ________."

4. Describe your home and the place where you live as if you were a creative writer.

5. Narrate the present moment and the experiences you're going through.

6. Breathe and allow the body to be still and relaxed throughout the meditation.

DAY 212

EXPERIMENTAL EXPERIENCES

"Experiences are the chemicals of life which the philosopher is experimenting with."

- Manly P. Hall -

DAY 213

COUNTING MEDITATION

Counting backward requires a little bit more concentration than counting forward, focus on maintaining mental alertness in this counting meditation.

1. Set your timer for five minutes or more.

2. Breathe in and out comfortably, allowing the body to be relaxed.

3. Begin counting down from 100, 99, 98....

4. Observe the thoughts that arise in the mind, and return to 100 when you lose count, beginning again.

5. Keep the mind alert and awake until your timer goes off.

DAY 214

AFFIRMATION FROM HEAD TO HEART

"When I begin to overthink, I take a deep breath

and drop into my heart, reconnecting with myself, reconnecting with the present."

DAY 215

RELAX AND ALLOW

Sometimes when we strive toward something we actually repel it. Meditate in deep stillness and silence today, letting go of any goals, ambitions, demands or dreams, Relax and allow the many seeds you've planted in your heart and mind to germinate.

DAY 216

COMMITMENT

Writing is a great way to become more aware of the thoughts that occur in our minds. Often, our thoughts move in and out so quickly that we don't always have the opportunity to really reflect on them.

Reflect today on your commitments.

1. On a blank sheet of paper, begin each line with the phrase, "I am committed to ________."

2. Write continuously for at least five minutes or until you've filled the page with your thoughts.

3. Reflect on the various commitments you've written out.

DAY 217

DRIFTWOOD IN A STREAM

Practice at least five minutes of mindfulness meditation today, being aware of the different thoughts as they arise in the mind.

1. Breathe mindfully, allowing the body to be very relaxed and still.

2. Observe the thoughts as they pass through your mind and allow them to drift past you, like driftwood floating in a stream.

3. Whenever a thought arises in the mind, silently say, "And there goes another one." bringing the awareness back to the breath.

DAY 218

AFFIRMATION FOR FLEXIBILITY

"Though I have many preferences, I am not limited by them. Though I have many goals, I am not limited by them. Though I have my desires, I am not limited by them."

DAY 219

TAKE YOUR OWN ADVICE

Often, we already know what to do but encounter layers of resistance preventing us from taking action. This meditation will help you connect to your own higher wisdom and take your own advice.

1. Take a moment to consider your most pressing challenge

2. Set a timer for at least five minutes, get into a comfortable position, and begin to meditate.

3. Envision yourself in a comfortable room sitting across from the highest version of yourself. They are in their best state, the best expression of you in every way.

4. With honesty and thoroughness, present to them the different aspects of your challenge.

5. Visualize them listening intently, Observe what they offer you in response and how that stems from your creative imagination.

6. When the timer goes off, write down the advice your higher self-gave you.

DAY 220

CLOUD GAZING

Recall your younger days when you might have looked up at the clouds to find formations in them. “That one looks like a dragon!” or “That one looks like a flower!” Take a moment today to look up at the sky and see what formations you find in the clouds.

DAY 221

ENCOURAGEMENT NOTES

To encourage means to "fill with courage," and courage is something that can get us through just about anything.

1. Make a list of five or more friends, family members, or acquaintances.

2. Write the, each a shot but thoughtful note of encouragement, -the more specific the better. Let them know the positive qualities you see in them and fill them with courage. You can text, email or handwrite the note.

3. Make sure they receive it today!

DAY 222

AFFIRMATION FOR FORGIVENESS

"I forgive others quickly and often. I apologize to others quickly and often. I forgive myself quickly and often. I apologize to myself quickly and often."

DAY 223

SOCIAL HOUSEKEEPING

We practice transforming the way we see the world, and we practice transforming the way we interact with the world. Part of that practice is recognizing the ways we may have harmed others and making an effort toward amends. Even if it's something small, a misunderstood statement or a careless act of dishonesty. -it can leave an energetic rift in our relationships.

1. Meditate and be extra compassionate with yourself.

2. Meditate on the personal characteristics that made it possible for harm to be done and be willing to overcome them

3. Visualize amends being made and breathe through it until it feels peaceful.

DAY 224

THEY KEY TO SUCCESS

"1 attribute my success to this. I never gave or took an excuse."

- Florence Nightingale -

DAY 225

EXPANSIVE BREATHS

1. Set a timer for at least five minutes, sit comfortably and close your eyes.

2. Take a deep breath into the lungs, stretching the lungs in all directions, top, bottom, left, right, front and back.

3. Hold for five...four...three...two...one…

4. Empty the lungs entirely on the exhale. Pushing all the air out

5. Hold for five...four...three...two...one…

6. Repeat filling and emptying the lungs until your timer goes off.

DAY 226

TIME TRAVEL AFFIRMATION

"What memory brings me joy? I can experience joy now. What memory brings me hope? I can experience hope now. What memory brings me

courage? I can experience courage now."

DAY 227

MEDITATION OF HEALING WATERS

1. Sit cross-legged or upright in a chair
2. Relax every muscle in the body with every exhale.
3. Observe your thoughts and the sounds. smells, and feelings you're experiencing now.
4. Visualize a waterfall of purifying water pouring down over the crown of your head, making its way into every cell of the inside of your body.
5. Envision this water saturating and filling the entire head and neck, upgrading everything in your brain.
6. Visualize this water moving down and filling every part of the spine and nervous system, healing and supercharging your physical body.

7. Imagine each and every organ and gland, tissue, muscle, bone and fluid in your body being washed and cleaned by the same water.

8. Let this feel very nourishing and relaxing as if this water is providing exactly what every part of the body needs.

9. Relax a little bit deeper and shine a little bit brighter with every exhale.

DAY 228

FORWARD FOLD

1. Stand up straight and extend your arms out straight to your left and to your right.

2. Take a deep breath in, and on your exhale, swan dive into a forward fold.

3. Allow your hands to touch the floor, if possible.

4. Let your head and neck rest under their own weight.

5. Take a few deep breaths on the forward fold.

6. Gradually begin to roll back up, one vertebra at a time.

7. Allow your upper back, shoulders, neck and head to be the very last parts of your body to come up.

DAY 229

GOOD VIBES TO THE UNIVERSE

1. Stand comfortably facing north, if possible, with your arms relaxed by your sides.

2. Close your eyes and take a deep breath into your heart center.

3. Envision your exhale sending loving energy from the front of your heart out into the universe endlessly. Take three deep breaths, everywhere sending love to the universe.

4. Step to turn your body to the left to face west. Take three deep breaths, the exhales blessing the universe with your goodness and compassion.

5. Rotate to the left gain, stepping and turning your body to face south. Take three deep breaths, exhaling love, just as before.

6. Rotate to the left again, facing east. Take three deep breaths, blessing the universe with your exhales

7. Place both hands over your heart as you rotate left once more, facing north in the same position as you begin. Say out loud, "Thank you. I love you"

DAY 230

AFFIRMATION FOR CURIOSITY

"To live in this world is to learn. I open my mind to learning new things. To love in this world is to transform, I open myself to new experiences. Today, I walk through this world with curiosity, with interest, and with non-attachment."

DAY 231

SURFACE SCAN

We often have hundreds of simultaneous sensations in various parts of the body at once. Today, we will become aware of each of them, holding an open awareness of the overall experience while also holding a focused awareness of each of them individually.

1. Take a seat in a comfortable position and set a time for at least 5 minutes.

2. Close your eyes and bring your awareness to your breath.

3. Mentally scan the surface of your skin from the top of your head all the way down over every part of your body.

4. Observe the sensations you feel in your environment, the experience of the air on your skin, your hair, clothing and so on.

5. Breathe comfortably and allow your body to be very relaxed.

6. Hold an open awareness of your overall experience while also moving through scanning every part of your body.

7. When your timer goes off, take a few deep breaths.

DAY 232

MINDFUL CHORES

Give yourself extra time to do your personal chores today. Be as deliberate and present as possible about the different aspects of these tasks, taking great care to be orderly, accurate, and thorough.

DAY 233

GOOD/BAD VERSUS ORDERLY/DISORDERLY

Practice non judgement by opening your mind to seeing things beyond judgmental analysis with a sense of curiosity and nuance.

A few examples of mindful spectrums of analysis are.

1. Mature/Immature
2. Knowledgeable/Ignorant
3. Orderly/Disorderly

What are some things that you think of as "bad"? Would it be possible to consider the possibility that they are actually the result of immaturity, ignorance or disorder? Journal your reflections on this.

DAY 234

AFFIRMATION FOR ORDER

"In my mind, my heart, and the world around me, there is a place for everything and all things find their place."

DAY 235

STICK WITH THE BREATH

Lie down and practice breath awareness meditation by putting your right hand over your heart center and your left hand over your navel.

1. Breathing in, silently say, "in...in….in…."
2. Breathing out, silently say, "out….out….out…."
3. Notice the thoughts that come to mind, but stick with the breath.

4. Hear the sounds and movements happening in all directions around you, but stick with the breath.

5. Observe the sensations on the body, but stick with the breath.

DAY 236

WEIGHT-SHIFTING BALANCE SITTING

1. Sit down with your back erect and both feet flat on the floor, setting a timer for five minutes.

2. Rest both hands flat down on your thighs.

3. Breathe comfortably and gently shift your weight to the left for three deep breaths.

4. Gently shift your weight back to the center and find your balance for three deep breaths.

5. Shift your weight to the right and take three deep breaths. Come back to center for three deep breaths.

6. Continue to shift your weight left, center, right, center, left etc. taking three breaths in each position until your timer goes off.

DAY 237

AFFIRMATION FOR ENTHUSIASM

"From deep within me arises a sense of enthusiasm. From deep within my heart arises zest for life. From deep within my mind arises vitality."

DAY 238

BEACH VACATION VISUALIZATION MEDITATION

Visualize yourself on a relaxing beach enjoying the warm sun and cool breeze. And your body can't help but begin to relax, as if you've been transported there. Give yourself a beach vacation meditation for at least five minutes.

DAY 239

STEADY WISH FOR ULTIMATE GOOD

"Love is not affectionate feeling but a steady wish for the loved person's ultimate good as far as it can be obtained."

- C. S. Lewis -

DAY 240

PERSPECTIVE SHIFT

Throughout your day, scan your surroundings and observe all the different things you can see your mind has layers and layers of existing thoughts and beliefs about every one of these things. As you observe the world today, silently repeat the following mantra. *"I am open to seeing things differently."*

DAY 241

MIRACULOUS UNIVERSE

The universe is more miraculous, surprising and dynamic than any of us could ever realize.

DAY 242

E PLURIBUS UNUM

It just requires one unique individual in a collective dynamic to bring order and collaboration to a time of confusion and discord. Today, in meditation, practice viewing the world from certain eyes. Set a timer for five minutes and softly echo the mantra "E Pluribus Unum," which means "out of many, one." Return to the refrain if the mind wanders. Enable a wave of relief to flow across any aspect of your body with each exhale, as though each exhale produces a wave of "order" in all directions around you.

DAY 243

AFFIRMATION FOR PRESENCE

"Throughout each day, I pause and check in with how I feel physically, emotionally and mentally."

DAY 244

FOREST VISUALIZATION

1. Close your eyes and set a timer for at least five minutes.

2. Visualize yourself sitting in the center of a beautiful forest.

3. As you breathe, “feel” that this is a safe, peaceful place for you to be.

4. Allow every exhale to take you deeper and deeper into relaxation.

5. Visualize beautiful flowers, butterflies, and hummingbirds surrounding you. See the sunlight shining through the trees.

6. Imagine the smell of cool moss and clean air.

7. Imagine that just being there is healing every part of your body, mind and spirit.

8. Notice any images that may arise in your mind as you challenge yourself to hold the visualization of the enchanted forest.

DAY 245

BLESSINGS ON BLESSINGS

Consider that any phrase you utter brings thousands of unseen foot soldiers out into the universe to do your bidding.

Imagine those foot soldiers doing just as you mean, except first to you and then to the planet around you.

Practice voicing life, liberation, and happiness into the universe by inspiring caring words of encouragement to anyone you meet today.

DAY 246

THE JOY OF UNDERSTANDING

"The noblest measure is the joy of understanding."

- Leonardo da Vinci -

DAY 247

BE KIND

"How will I be kinder today?" ask yourself.

DAY 248

MENTAL NOTING

1. Get comfortable and begin to meditate.

2. As you breathe, allow your exhales to bring deep relaxation.

3. Settle into a sense of stillness, softening any rigidity.

4. Observe the thoughts passing through your mind.

5. Mentally narrate thoughts, noting them as they arise. "Now I notice a thought about _____"

6. Always bring your awareness back to the breath after you note a thought, each exhale should take you deeper into relaxation.

DAY 249

PSYCHIC DEVELOPMENT

Thinking symbolically and metaphorically has long been considered the way prophets and psychics get their information. In this mindful writing exercise, reflect on the following prompts.

1. In the most encouraging way possible, if I were a car, what kind of car would I be, and why?

2. In the most encouraging way possible, if I were an animal, what kind of animal would I be, and why?

3. In the most encouraging way possible, if I were a song, what song would I be, and why?

DAY 250

SELF-COMPASSION MEDITATION

There is a collective mesmerism that has us convinced that we aren't good enough, smart enough, beautiful enough… or that we are simply "not enough". Break the spell! Meditate today using the following mantra. *"I am worthy of happiness, health and wealth."*

1. Get comfortable

2. Silently repeat the mantra with every inhale and every exhale

3. Observe your thoughts, overriding anything that comes up by always repeating the mantra with every inhale and every exhale.

4. Meditate for at least five minutes.

DAY 251

AFFIRMATION FOR MINDFUL ATTITUDE

"My outlook on life is positive, curious, and non-judgmental. I cultivate an outlook on life that is positive, curious, and non-judgmental. I am positive, curious, and non-judgmental."

DAY 252

BE THE OBJECT

Cultivate a sense of connectedness to your surroundings today.

Choose an object, -it can be any household object, and this will be the focus of your open-eye meditation today.

1. Sit or stand comfortably in front of the object and set a timer for five or more minutes.

2. Allow your gaze to rest comfortably on the object. When your gaze moves from the object, bring it back.

3. Allow the muscles in your face and shoulders to relax and soften under their own weight.

4. Observe the thoughts, emotions, or physical sensations that may arise, breathing through them.

5. Imagine that the space between you and the object is not empty space at all, but that is an atmospheric field holding you and the object together in a greater container.

6. Imagine that you are the object, and the object is part of you.

7. Breathe, letting go of any sense of strain.

DAY 253

POWER POSES

In a private place, practice power posing. Envision a superhero, how they stand with their hands on their hips and their chest out, gazing confidently off into the distance. This body language can send a powerful message to your unconscious mind and even release confidence-boosting hormones.

Focus on boosting your own confidence by power posing in private. Remember this exercise for your next job interview, difficult conversation, or audition.

DAY 254

EMOTIONAL BODY

Get to know your body's relationships to your emotions. Choose three emotions to work with, one positive like joy, one negative like frustration, and one neutral like indifference.

1. Settle into meditation, allowing the body to be very relaxed.

2. Begin with the negative emotion. Bring it to mind and notice the energy as it moves into the body. Observe what parts of the body

react and activate. DO not stay here ling, but take a few breaths to observe the experience.

3. Move to your neutral emotion. Breathe and allow it to wash over you. Observe the body. What does the neutral emotion feel like?

4. Finally, bring up your positive emotion. Fill your heart, body, and mind with it. How does it feel in the body?

DAY 255

BUILDING CONFIDENCE

Ask yourself, *"What do I need to do to feel more confident?"* Listen to your heart's response.

DAY 256

PAY IT FORWARD

Reflect on the people in your life who make you feel loved and supported. In what ways do they do this? How can you "pay it forward" by offering those same gifts to them and others?

DAY 257

LOVE THEM

"If you judge people, you have no time to love them."

- Mother Teresa

DAY 258

MIND AND BODY CONNECTION

Develop a deeper mind and moody connection while exploring natural curiosity. Get into a comfortable position and set your timer for at least five minutes for this purpose.

1. Ask yourself, *"If my thoughts could change my body, what thoughts would I think?"*

2. Observe the natural response your mind offers up

3. Take a deep breath, and allow your body to relax.

4. Ask yourself the same question again.

5. Observe your mind's response and keep breathing

6. Continue to ask the same question, allowing the body to remain relaxed and still, observing the mind's natural responses.

DAY 259

AFFIRMATION FOR DEPTH

"There is more to know than I can see on the surface, so I am patient. There is more to learn that can be spoken with words, so I open my mind. There is more to experience than can ever be realized, so I open my heart."

DAY 260

BIG SIGH

Check in with how you feel before meditating.

1. Relax into a comfortable position and set a timer for at least five minutes.

2. Let all the muscles on your body become still and go soft.

3. Breathe into the top, bottom, left, right, front and back of the lungs. Exhaling with a gentle but audible sighing sound.

4. Consciously inhale into all directions as before and consciously exhale with a sight every single time until your timer goes off.

Check in with how you feel after meditating.

DAY 261

IT'S TOTALLY POSSIBLE!

Let go of mental limitations and open your mind to new possibilities in this journaling exercise. Practice stream of consciousness journaling, which means writing without pausing or thinking about what you're writing.

1. Close your eyes and take a few deep breaths

2. Consider a few things you'd like to experience that may seem outrageous or impossible.

3. Set a timer for at least five minutes.

4. Take out a clean sheet of paper and practice stream of consciousness journaling, starting each line with. “It’s totally possible that….”

DAY 262

PRACTICAL TELEPATHY

Imagine that there is no such thing as a private though, that on some level every human being has access to everyone’s thoughts.

Visualize sending the following positive thoughts into the minds of every living person in the world.

“May all of us have all that we need. May all of us be loved in the ways that are just right. May all of us know what to do next in our lives. May all of us be forgiven of our faults and shortcomings. May all of us be healed in every possible way.”

DAY 263

ANCESTOR LOVINGKINDNESS MEDITATION

World traditions suggest purifying our relationship with the family members who came before us. Practice a loving-kindness meditation today to heal, love and forgive and offer gratitude to your ancestors.

1. Sit comfortably with both your hands resting open, palms up.

2. Breathe comfortably and let your body relax.

3. Cultivate a sense of open-heartedness, acceptance, and gratitude for who you are and all your blessings.

4. Next, visualize your parents. Welcome them into your heart with an energetic field of lovingkindness and honor. Observe what thoughts and feelings arise.

5. Until your timer goes off, continue, cultivating, loving kindness as you visualize your many ancestors one by one.

DAY 264

THE EYE OF THE BEHOLDER

It is said that beauty is in the eye of the beholder. Move throughout your day today finding beauty in everything.

DAY 265

WISDOM OF ZOROASTER

"Taking the first footstep with the good though, the second with the good word, and the third with the good deed, I entered paradise."

- Zoroaster -

DAY 266

RAINBOW RESET

Every color is associated with different feelings, emotions and experience. Meditate on each color of the rainbow for a full spectrum reset, cultivating a sense of peacefulness and observing the different mental associations that come up.

1. Set a timer for at least five minutes, close your eyes, and get into a comfortable position.

2. Allow every exhale to bring a wave of relaxation through all the muscles in the body.

3. Become aware of any emotions, thoughts, or sensations you are experiencing.

4. Visualize red light filling your mind and body. Notice what comes up. Take three deep breaths.

5. Visualize orange, yellow, green, blue, indigo, and violet, taking three deep breaths at each color, observing your mind and body.

DAY 267

RIGHT ON SCHEDULE

Consider the possibility that you are in the exact right place at the exact right time and that your extraordinary destiny is unfolding exactly according to plan.

DAY 268

AFFIRMATION FOR POWER

"My thoughts are very powerful. I choose them wisely. My words are very powerful. I choose them wisely. My actions are very powerful. I choose them wisely."

DAY 269

MINDFUL LISTENING VARIATION

1. Find a comfortable standing position and allow your arms to rest naturally at your side and close your eyes.

2. With your right hand, gently plug your right ear, and listen closely with your left ear.

3. Take three deep breaths in and out, listening.

4. Lower your right arm, and using your left hand, gently plug your left ear. Listen closely with your right ear, taking three deep breaths in and out.

5. Notice the subtle differences in what each ear hears.

6. Alternate Between the ears and three times each, staying as relaxed as possible throughout the process.

7. Let both arms rest to your side. Take three deep breaths, relaxing every part of the body and listening with both ears, observing the experience with non judgement and total awareness.

DAY 270

WEATHER REPORT

1. Get comfortable and begin meditating.

2. Observe how you're feeling physically, mentally and emotionally.

3. Give yourself a weather report of how you're feeling. "Physically I'm feeling energized and strong like a warm summer day, but emotionally and mentally. I'm feeling a little scattered and frustrated like a dark thunderstorm."

DAY 271

AFFIRMATION FOR PERSONAL PERCEPTION TRANSFORMATION

"I am open to seeing myself differently. I am willing to see myself differently. I am determined to see

myself differently"

DAY 272

IMPERIUM

Mindfulness practices help us establish a sense of power or authority over our automatic behaviors, developing a greater sense of confidence and self-control. Meditate for at least five minutes. Silently. Repeating the mantra "Imperium." Which means "Power" or "Authority". When the mind wanders, come back to the mantra.

With each exhale, allow a wave of relaxation to pass through every part of the body, as if each exhale is establishing greater power throughout every part of your being.

DAY 273

THE ONE WHO I AM

"The one who I am is more powerful than the one I desire to be. The one who I am is more meaningful than the one I strive to be, The one who I am is more lovable than the one I pretend to be."

DAY 274

THE WORLD OF DREAMS

"Once day it will have to be officially admitted that what we have christened reality is an even greater illusion than the world of dreams."

- Salvador Dali -

DAY 275

I REALLY APPRECIATE

Move throughout your day with a practice of open awareness and a sense of gratitude for things you may normally overlook. Cultivate appreciation for the little things and speak your appreciation out loud to yourself or to those around you, silently repeating the mantra. "I really appreciate _________." Fill in the blank with various people and things you are grateful for.

DAY 276

AFFIRMATION FOR HAPPINESS

"I'm happy with who I am and grateful for who I'm becoming. I'm happy with the life I love and grateful for the life I'm building. I'm happy with the relationships I have and grateful for the deepened connections I'm creating."

DAY 277

LETTING GO OF ATTACHMENT TO OUTCOMES

1. Get comfortable, set a timer for at least five minutes, and begin to meditate.

2. As you breathe, exhale into deep relaxation.

3. Settle into a sense of relaxed stillness.

4. Observe the specific thoughts, images, and ideas passing through your mind.

5. Identify a specific thought or idea as it arises and tell yourself. "I have attachments about __, but I am willing to let them go and see things differently."

6. Bring your awareness back to the breath and identity the next though that comes up, repeating the statement until the timer goes off.

DAY 278

DUSTING OFF OLD ENERGY

1. Stand in a comfortable position and take a few deep breaths.

2. Using your hands, brush any negative or stale energy off your body, as if you were brushing off dust, with swift strokes.

3. Breathe out with every stroke

4. Brush off your shoulders, your arms, your back, torso, and legs.

DAY 279

GREAT HEIGHTS

Train yourself to see things from a bird's eye view.

1. Lie down in a comfortable position with your arms resting at your sides and set a timer for five minutes.

2. Close your eyes and allow the body to relax.

3. Visualize looking down at yourself from up above.

4. Consider the thoughts and circumstances that preoccupy your life today.

5. Gradually allow your visualization to expand, as you look down upon yourself from greater and greater heights.

6. Notice how your challenges become smaller the higher you go.

When you're ready to finish the exercise, journal any insight that may come up for you around specific challenges you face.

DAY 280

AFFIRMATION FOR AUTHENTICITY

"I allow myself to think for myself, I allow myself to speak for myself. I allow myself to be myself."

DAY 281

TONING AHHH….

Take a few minutes to practice toning mantra meditation.

1. Get into a comfortable position and close your eyes.

2. Allow your breaths to be expansive and full, breathing deeply on the inhales and emptying the lungs completely on the exhales.

3. Release an open-mouth tone for the entire out breath. "Ahh…."

4. Keep the tone and note consistent throughout the exhale.

5. Focus your attention on the experience of the vibration throughout your body.

6. Imagine the sound vibrations passing through every cell in your body and echoing in all directions around you.

DAY 282

EXERCISE FOR SEEING THINGS DIFFERENTLY

1. Get into a comfortable position, close your eyes, and take a few deep breaths to relax.

2. Rub your hands together and then hold them over your eyes.

3. Notice the warmth of your hands through your eyelids.

4. Imagine that the energy from your hands is healing your eyes, recalibrating your vision, and opening perspective.

5. Take a few deep breaths with your hands over your eyes. Repeat a few times, allowing yourself to become more and more relaxed and more open to "seeing" things differently.

DAY 283

DNA ACTIVATION VISUALIZATION MEDITATION

We carry all the genetic information necessary for a perfectly healthy and strong body. In this meditation we will merge mind and matter in an exercise to activate our highest potential through allowing it to merge.

1. Set a timer for at least five minutes, begin to meditate, and allow the body to relax deeply.

2. Visualize your double helix DNA and envision it as it moves throughout every part of your body.

3. Gradually releasing all the tension in your body, imagine your DNA radiating bright light.

4. Imagine that this bright light is activating the highest possible expression of your genetic potential.

5. Visualize your body getting stronger and healthier, your mind getting clearer and sharper, and your immune system becoming more invincible."

DAY 284

AFFIRMATION FOR TRUST

"I recognize that nothing is certain in this world, and I am not alone in that uncertainty. I move through life knowing that all living beings are in this together, and I trust that this is a loving

universe with loving intentions, designed for my ultimate good."

DAY 285

INSIGHT MEDITATION

Practice the discipline of open awareness, using the breath as the anchor

1. Sit in a comfortable position, set a timer for at least five minutes, and allow all the muscles in the body to relax.

2. Close your eyes and bring your mental focus to the upper lip as you breathe in and out your nose.

3. Observe the automatic behavior of the mind, witness the thoughts, ideas and images, that arise and then bring the attention back to the sensation of the breath on the upper lip.

4. Continue until your timer goes off.

DAY 286

STRENGTH AND FLEXIBILITY WRITING EXERCISE

Imagine your great-great-grandchildren, as your audience and write a description of what you are experiencing in life. Be mindful of the subtle implications of your word choices, but be truthful and inspiring.

Ask yourself, *"How can I rewrite the current story of my life from a powerful and enlightened perspective, navigating the greatest challenges of my time with strength and flexibility?"*

DAY 287

CHEERFULNESS MEDITATION

Cultivating a sense of cheerfulness and joy in our lives can provide great power to overcome tricky circumstances. Cheer and joy are not the result of circumstances, they themselves are decisions and habits to be developed

1. Set a timer for at least five minutes, get into a comfortable position, and begin to meditate.

2. Breathing in and out, become loose and comfortable in your body.

3. Bring to mind images of children laughing and playing.

4. Smile and allow your inhales to bring that joyful energy into your present moment.

5. Notice the sensations in the body and the information that arises in the mind.

Consciously cultivate cheer and joy, carrying it with you wherever you go today.

DAY 288

RESPONSIBILITY FOR ALL HUMANITY

Each of us must work for his own improvement, and at the same time share a general responsibility for all humanity, our particular duty being to aid those to whom we think we can be most useful. - Marie Curie

DAY 289

RECALIBRATING ASSOCIATIONS

Relax and allow your gaze to movie around the room or space you are in now. Open your mind to seeing things differently through practicing mindful observation. Glance around at everything, not excluding anything in particular and not focusing on anything specific either, silently saying to yourself. "There are existing associations in my mind, which I am open to updating". When your gaze rests upon one object, repeat the mantra and allow your gaze to move to another object. Practice this for at least five minutes.

DAY 290

MUSCLE ENERGIZATION

Energize every muscle group in your body by gently activating it.

Stand up for this practice and make sure to take full, deep inhales and complete exhales throughout the process.

1. Begin by opening and stretching the fingers on both hands and clenching both fists.

2. Rotate your wrists, neck, hips, and ankles in both directions.

3. Flex and stretch the muscles in your arms, chest, back, core and legs.

4. Roll your shoulders, and bring awareness into the body, stretching, flexing and relaxing every muscle you can think of.

DAY 291

VESSEL FOR KINDNESS BODY SCAN

Send the message to your body that it is dedicated to kindness and compassion. Program and receive deeply the idea that this body exists to be a vessel for giving and receiving kindness.

1. Recline or lie down comfortably.

2. Close your eyes and take a few deep breaths.

3. Sweep your awareness to each and every part of your body and begin with your feet all the way up to your head.

4. Silently say, "You are here to express kindness in infinite ways."

5. Imagine a portal of infinite kindness, deep in the center of every atom that makes up every part of your body and allow that kindness to fill every part of you and shine all around you.

DAY 292

PLEASE AND THANK YOU BREATHWORK

Cultivate a sense of power and gratitude by practicing conscious breathwork. This entails three simultaneous components.

1. Breathing consciously, one inhale into the belly, a second inhale into the chest and then a full exhale.

2. Letting the body become completely relaxed, signaling to the nervous system that old patterns can be cleared.

3. Silently repeating the phrase, "Please and thank you" with the breath like so "Please" on the belly inhale, "and" on the chest inhale, and "thank you," on the exhale.

Set a timer for five minutes and practice this breathwork exercise until your timer goes off. Then take three deep breaths and set an intention for yourself.

DAY 293

HEALING FLAME MEDITATION

1. Visualize a white spark of healing fire behind your eyes in the very center of your brain.

2. Envision this white flame becoming larger and brighter, filling the head and neck, purifying every thought, memory, and idea in your mind.

3. Visualize this white flame moving down and filling the spine and nervous system, nourishing and upgrading your physical body, purifying old patterns, habits, and memories.

4. Imagine each and every organ and gland, tissue, muscle, bone and fluid in your body ablaze with this same white flame.

5. Let the flame nourish and relax you, as if this fire is providing exactly what every part of the body needs.

6. Relax just a little bit deeper with every breath and see the flame burn a little bit brighter with every exhale.

DAY 294

CALM AND BALANCED

1. Set a timer for about five minutes,

2. Stand comfortably and let your body relax.

3. Hold your hands against your heart center or pressed together as in a prayer.

4. Lift your right leg by bending your knee and place your right foot on your left calf, balancing on your left foot.

5. Take three deep breaths in and out before lowering your right foot to the floor and balancing your left foot on your right calf for three breaths.

6. Continue balancing on each foot, taking three call, deep breaths each time, until your timer goes off.

DAY 295

TIME TRAVEL AND UNCONDITIONAL LOVE

1. Set a timer for at least five minutes and sit comfortably.

2. Recall one of your earliest and most significant memories.

3. Visualize yourself time travelling back to that moment.

4. Imagine that you are able to communicate directly with your past self in that moment.

5. Encourage, inspire, and forgive them with the wisdom you've gained since then.

6. Offer your past self-unconditional acceptance and love.

DAY 296

AFFIRMATION FOR NON ATTACHMENT

"The universe is in constant motion. I am part of the universe, so I too am in constant motion, constant motion means constant change and this is perfectly natural. IT is in my nature to constantly

adapt to change. I am open to infinite outcomes and I celebrate uncertainty."

DAY 297

TELEPATHIC INTERPLAY

Imagine invisible vibrations of energy and tubes of light pulsating in all directions, filling all the empty space surrounding everyone and everything. Every thought we think is vibrational energy transmitted and received consciously and unconsciously.

DAY 298

LETTERS OF HOPE

Consider someone in your life who is going through a hard time.

With love and generosity, write a message of hope to them. When you are finished, sign the letter, tear it up, and throw it away, imagining that the message of hope is being released into the universe.

DAY 299

PRESENT MOMENT CONTEXT

Cultivate a more advanced expression of present moment context by expanding your awareness beyond your surroundings in this meditation.

1. Set a timer for your meditation.

2. Close your eyes and bring the awareness into the breath.

3. Visualize yourself in your current environment, seeing all directions around you.

4. Welcome the sensations in your body, your emotions, and anything else that presents itself to you.

5. Visualize the immediate surroundings, the building and neighborhood you are in, expanding outward to the city, nation, planet, and beyond until your timer goes off.

DAY 300

INTEGRITY

"The most important persuasion tool you have in your entire arsenal is integrity."

\- Zig Ziglar -

DAY 301

DESIRE INSIGHT MEDITATION

We are so often in unconscious pursuit of our desires that we rarely stop to ask ourselves why we want what we think we want.

1. Take a few minutes to meditate and ask yourself, "What do I want?"

2. Notice your mind's first natural response.

3. Consider the response and ask yourself, "Why do I want it?"

4. Notice your mind's natural response.

5. Journal a few paragraphs about desire, your relationships with it, and what meditation showed you about why you may want it.

DAY 302

EMOTIONAL INVENTORY

Take out a journal or a blank sheet of paper. Write out at least one full page of whatever emotions you are currently experiencing,

Imagine that no one will ever see this. List whatever you're feeling, take a full inventory of whatever comes up, and save it for yourself to reflect on for insight at another time.

DAY 303

PULCHRA MOMENTUM

Embrace the present moment by meditating with the mantra "Pulchra Momentum." which means "Beautiful moment".

DAY 304

HANDWASHING MEDITATION

Make washing your hands a meditation.

1. Take a few deep breaths and experience the temperature of the water.

2. Really notice the fragrance of the soap, massaging it into your hands.

3. Mindfully clean every part of the hands, between fingers, underneath the fingernails.

DAY 305

AFFIRMATION FOR ACCEPTANCE

"I accept myself as I am, knowing that I am always changing, I accept others as they are, knowing that they are always changing, I accept circumstances as they are, knowing that they are always changing."

DAY 306

THIS IS YOUR GENERATION

Every individual in a generation is the co-creator of that generation's history.

1. Begin your meditation by setting a timer for five minutes and getting into a comfortable position.

2. Silently repeat the statement, "I am a co-creator of my generation, and history will remember my contributions.'

3. When your timer goes off, stretch the body in any way that feels comfortable for you.

4. Take a deep breath and say out loud, "I am a co-creator of my generation, and history will remember my contributions."

DAY 307

UPLIFTING PLAYLIST

Create a playlist of music that feels and sounds uplifting. Consider lyrics, sound, rhythm, and the energy you feel when you listen to the songs.

DAY 308

REVERENCE INSIGHT MEDITATION

Reverence is deep respect for the sacred, and from a mindfulness perspective, all beings and all things are worthy of reverence.

1. Take a few minutes to meditate and set a timer for at least five minutes.

2. Ask yourself, “what does it mean for me to be reverent?”

3. Notice your mind’s natural response. Breathe and take your time.

4. Ask again, “What does it mean for me to be reverent?”

5. Allow the body to be relaxed as you continue to ask the same question, observing the many ways your mind will respond.

DAY 309

THE GREATEST BLESSING

"A wise man should consider that health is the greatest of human blessings and learn how by his own thought to derive benefit from his illnesses."

- Hippocrates -

DAY 310

MASTERFUL LIFESTYLE

All of life's experiences can be likened to the initiations for the martial artists. Sometimes one move must be practiced over and over and over again until it is mastered in order to achieve one degree of initiation. A masterful martial artist becomes so through discipline and consistency. Laziness or complacency has no place in the life of the martial artist, who maintains great order and commitment in daily life. Throughout your day, hold yourself to a higher standard.

Practice what you know to be true. Become masterful.

DAY 311

EVEN THIS IS A MEDITATION

Become very present wherever you are with whatever you're doing.

Bring your attention to the different components of your experience, treating the uncomfortable situations exactly the same as you treat comfortable situations. Throughout your day, silently repeat the mantra. "Even this is a meditation.". Observe any changes in your attitude, perception, or experience.

DAY 312

OPEN TO GUIDANCE

Sometimes, we can find ourselves at the end of one season, uncertain about the next. Other times we are faced with challenging decisions to make, or we feel at a loss for what to do next.

For today's meditation, use the mantra, "I am open to guidance."

There is great power in humility, and you will attract guidance just through your openness.

DAY 313

AFFIRMATION FOR NON JUDGEMENT

"I look upon others, their personalities, their shortcomings, and their process with understanding and compassion. I look upon myself, my personality, my shortcomings, and my process with understanding and compassion."

DAY 314

EVERYTHING MOVES, EVERYTHING VIBRATES

1. Lie down flat on your back with your palms facing up.

2. On your inhale, breathe into the top and the bottom, the left, and the right, and the front and the back sides of the lungs.

3. On your exhale, breathe out from the top and the bottom, the left and the right, and the front and the back sides of the lungs.

4. Bring your awareness to the vibration of your heartbeat.

5. Envision every cell in your being echoing its own heartbeat.

DAY 315

SOCIAL MEDIA CLEANUP

Social media can be a place where we receive great inspiration. But it can also be a place where we encounter ideas and images that don't support a lovingkindness lifestyle.

1. Take a few minutes to review the content you typically consume on your favorite social media platform.

2. Notice the types of posts on the accounts you follow.

3. Mute or unfollow any accounts presenting content that doesn't support the life you are trying to create.

DAY 316

PROGRESSIVE BREATHING

Meditate for at least five minutes today.

1. Close your eyes, and breathe in through the nose and out through the mouth, slowly and gradually never holding the breath.

2. Count to three as you inhale.

3. Count to three as you exhale

4. Count to five with each inhale and exhale.

5. Then count to seven with each inhale and exhale and then back to three.

6. Rotate through counting for three, then five, and then seven on both inhale and exhale until five minutes have passed.

DAY 317

"YES, AND…."

It is possible to disagree with someone without being disagreeable.

Practice positive communication through the "Yes, and…." technique.

1. Throughout your day, notice if you ever want to disagree with someone.

2. Consider if it is possible to integrate their perspective into your own.

3. When responding, practice positive communication by saying.

"Yes, and ______." adding your opinion to what they've presented rather than as a replacement.

DAY 318

FIDEM

Moving through life with a sense of faith provides an invisible power and momentum to whatever we are committed to. Meditate today using the mantra, "Fidem," which means "faith." "confidence," and "belief."

DAY 319

UNPROVOKABLE

Ask yourself today, *"Am I genuinely willing to stand strong in a place of peace, unprovoked by challenging circumstances.?"*

DAY 320

THE FEELING OF SOUND

1. Take a set, get comfortable, and begin your meditation by listening.

2. Imagine that you can feel every sound you hear in all directions.

3. In your mind's eye, envision the sound waves as they invisibly travel through the environment.

4. Observe the physical sensations in your body, Can you "feel" the sounds? Does your body have subtle reactions to sounds? What does it feel like?

DAY 321

AFFIRMATION FOR DISCERNMENT

"Things are not always as they seem on the surface,

so I am willing to take a deep breath and take a deeper look."

DAY 322

DANCING THROUGH LIFE

1. Get comfortable and begin to meditate

2. As you breathe, allow your exhales to bring deep relaxation.

3. Welcome the thoughts passing through your mind, observing them with curiosity.

4. As you relax deeper with every exhale, notice the rigidity melting away.

5. Visualize the different circumstances you're experiencing in life, and see them as moving oscillating, geometric forms twisting and turning like the energetic dynamics of a weather system.

6. Imagine that anything and everything can be moved through with balance, as if you were dancing

DAY 323

WHAT WE REMEMBER

"I've learned that people will forget what you said, people will forget what you did, but people will never forget how you made them feel."

- Maya Angelou -

DAY 324

KNOW THYSELF

The Greek aphorism "know thyself" was said to be written on the temple of Apollo, the god of light. Light is associated with knowledge and understanding. Ask yourself. "What can I learn about myself today.?"

DAY 325

HEART-HEALING ENERGY BALL

1. Sit or stand comfortably and let all the muscles in your body relax,

2. Cup your hands as if you're making a snowball, but don't let your two hands touch.

3. Breathe in and out, visualizing the exhale bringing energy from your head down through your hands.

4. Envision a vortex of positive healing energy being cultivated inside your hands.

5. Observe any sensations inside of your hands.

6. Place the energy ball into your heart center, smiling, and taking a few deep breaths to receive the healing energy in your heart.

DAY 326

ILLUMINATUS

Perhaps today you will become awakened to new levels of understanding, new clarity, new enlightenment. Meditate using the mantra, "Illuminatus" today which means "Illuminated", "clarified" or "enlightened" Silently repeat the mantra. When the mind is thinking anything but the mantra, notice it, and come back to the mantra.

DAY 327

AFFIRMATION FOR INDIVIDUALITY

"My perspective and opinion are valuable. Every person on this plant is an original, but not everyone chooses to express their originality. I choose to express mine. My uniqueness is my strength."

DAY 328

CHARACTER REFLECTION MEDITATION

1. Get into a comfortable position, set a timer for five minutes or more, and begin to meditate.

2. Start by bringing the awareness to the breath and letting the body relax.

3. Begin to reflect on your life, imagining that every moment of your life is a scene in a movie.

4. Imagine that every moment was a part of character development for your character in a movie.

5. Ponder the implications of your character. What kind of insight can you gain?

DAY 329

HEART OPENER

1. Stand up straight with your feet shoulder width apart.

2. Interlace your fingers behind your back with your palms touching and straighten your arms.

3. Lift your arms up behind your back with your psalm touching and straighten your arms.

4. Close your eyes and tilt your head as if you were looking up at the ceiling.

5. Take a few deep breaths and imagine your heart opening.

DAY 330

OVERCOMING DIFFICULT EMOTIONS

In meditation, we can reflect on things that challenge us in our loves with great power because in meditation we have the "home court" advantage over those challenges. When they come up in life, they can surprise us, but in meditation, we can call them forth to deal with them.

1. Take a seat and set a timer for at least five minutes.

2. Bring to mind a challenging person, place or thing.

3. Breathe into it and notice the different thoughts and feelings you have around it.

4. With every exhale, release the old ways of feeling, clearing through the discomfort

5. Imagine that the next time you are faced with this challenge in life, you are stronger, more stable, and less affected by it.

DAY 331

TRUTH AND CURIOSITY

"Truth does not appease but inflames the curiosity."

- Joseph Smith Jr. -

DAY 332

ELIMINATING DISTRACTIONS

In meditation, something is only a distraction if you deem it as such. Allow everything to be as it is, cultivating a sense of equanimity. We eliminate distractions by allowing them to become part of the meditation.

DAY 333

MAGNAE SOPHIA

Wisdom comes through experience and depth of understanding.

Meditation will help us make wise decisions and cultivate wise perspectives. Meditate today using the mantra "Magnae Sophia," which means "great wisdom."

DAY 334

COUNTING BY TWO MEDITATION

Practice maintaining mental alertness by counting by two.

1. Set a timer for five minutes or more

2. Breathe in and out comfortably, allowing the body to be relaxed.

3. Begin counting by two: two….four….six….eight….10

4. Observe the thoughts that arise in the mind and return to two when you lose count or reach 100.

5. Keep the mind alert and awake until your timer goes off.

DAY 335

AFFIRMATION FOR COURAGE

"I trust my strength, my endurance, and my decisions. I know that I am strong enough to make it through any challenge presented to me. If it is meant to be, there will be a way."

DAY 336

CLOUDS IN THE SKY

1. Set a timer for five minutes or more. Breathe mindfully allowing the body to be very relaxed and still.

2. Observe the thoughts as they pass through your mind, and allow them to drift on by, like clouds in the sky on a clear day.

3. Remain relaxed and still in the body until your timer goes off.

DAY 337

PRACTICE WHAT YOU KNOW

"Practice what you know, and it will help to make clear what now you do not know."

- Rembrandt -

DAY 338

INTENTION CHECKING

Sometimes we have a superficial intention, but layers of other intentions exist beneath the surface. Meditate using the following questions as a mantra "What are my intentions?" Observe the thoughts that arise in the mind in automatic response as you continue to ask that question/

DAY 339

AFFIRMATION FOR INSIGHT

DAY 340

I AM ABUNDANT IN

The abundance of the universe is yours for the taking! Recalibrate your awareness to the abundance that already surrounds you as an exercise to cultivate gratitude.

1. Have a seat, close your eyes, and take a few deep breaths.

2. Make a mental inventory of the abundance of your experience.

3. Write a list in your journal, itemizing various areas you experience abundance, using the structure "I am abundant in…."

DAY 341

MINDFUL MEMORY RECOLLECTION

Mindful memory recollection is about remembering situations based on your current state of consciousness. Reflect on the following writing prompts.

1. How have I described this situation in the past?

2. How might I describe this situation with a new perspective?

DAY 342

BOX BREATH

1. Set a timer for at least five minutes, sit comfortably, and close your eyes.

2. Take a deep breath into the lungs, stretching them in all directions, and breathing in for a count of four… three… two…. One…

3. Hold your full lungs for a count of four… three… two…. One…

4. Empty the lungs entirely on the exhale, releasing any stale energy and exhaling for a count of four… three… two…. One…

5. Hold your empty lungs for a count of four… three… two…. One…

6. Continue until your timer goes off.

DAY 343

AFFIRMATION FOR EMPATHY

"I see myself in the eyes of others. We are all reflections of one another."

DAY 344

ON THE ALTAR

We are often confused or threatened by the circumstances of our lives, whether they are confusion, mutual problems, or almost insurmountable targets. In the past, we might put something of immense importance or concern on the altar as a gift, so that the divine forces of the world might "alter," render them permanent, or intensify them. Remember your obstacles, questions, and aspirations for a moment. Place them on the metaphorical "altar" in order for them to be supernaturally "altered."

DAY 345

WINGSPAN BALANCE CALF RAISES

1. Extend your arms straight out to your left and to your right, fingers together and palms facing forward.

2. Slowly shift your weight onto the balls of your feet, lifting your heels off the ground, flexing your calves as you rise.

3. Take three deep breaths, maintaining your balance.

4. Slowly bring your heels back to the ground, relaxing your calves. Take three deep breaths before rising up again.

5. Repeat for five minutes.

DAY 346

THE MAGIC OF CEREMONY

Ceremony is when we bring words, movement, and intention together to generate a spiritual psychological or social experience.

Consider that many things in our lives are already ceremonial, and open your mind to ways that the magic of ceremony can enhance your everyday life.

DAY 347

FOLLOW THROUGH

"The immature mind hops from one thing to another, the mature mind seeks to follow through."

- Harry Allen Overstreet -

DAY 348

SPIRIT OF PROSPERITY

Prosperity is an energetic spirit and experience that is not dependent on physical evidence.

1. Set a timer for at least five minutes.

2. Get into a comfortable position.

3. Silently repeat the following mantra to yourself throughout your meditation: "In what ways do I already experience prosperity?"

4. Notice any thoughts or feelings that arise, allowing a wave of relaxation to pass through every muscle group with every exhale.

DAY 349

AFFIRMATION FOR CREATIVITY

"I give myself permission to be accessible to fresh concepts and feelings. I know what I want to do, and I let my imagination guide me there. My mind is brimming with ideas, and I am careful with my imaginative process."

DAY 350

DRAWING ENERGY UP THE SPINE

1. Sit cross-legged or upright in a chair and set a timer for five or more minutes.

2. Relax every muscle in the body with every exhale.

3. Direct your awareness to the base of your spine, envisioning a pool of energy there.

4. With every inhale, imagine that energy gradually spiraling up the spine, slowly emerging from the crown of your head like a fountain of energy showering you in light.

5. With every exhale, allow a wave of relaxation to pass from the top of the body down into the ground.

6. Practice this visualization until your timer goes off.

DAY 351

MEALTIME BLESSING

Turn your mealtime into a meditation by dedication your meals to the strengthening and nourishment of your body.

1. Have a seat at the table with your meal in front of you.

2. Before you take your first bit, hold your plate or bowl in both hands and close your eyes.

3. Visualize a bright white light shining down through the crown of your head, toward your heart, and through your hands into the food.

4. Imagine that this light is transforming the cells of the food, transforming the food into exactly what your body needs.

5. When you're ready, open your eyes, look at the meal, and say out loud, "I am so thankful for this food!"

6. Enjoy your meal.

DAY 352

AFFIRMATION FOR WISDOM

"Just because I see, think or hear something doesn't mean it's real, true or relevant. Just because I can't see or understand something doesn't mean it's less real, true, or relevant."

DAY 353

ENERGY HEALING

1. Set a timer for at least five minutes, lie down in a comfortable position, and close your eyes

2. Cultivate a sense of love by thinking of loved ones.

3. Visualize healing energetic light moving down through the crown of your head toward your heart and releasing from your hands.

4. Set an intention for healing and place your hands on the top of your head, over your face, your arms, your heart, your belly and beyond.

5. Take your time with each placement, not rushing the process.

DAY 354

INSPIRED INTERPRETATION OF THE PRESENT

We often don't see things as they are, but rather, as "we" are. Practice describing the present moment in a new way, cultivating an inspired interpretation of it.

1. Sit comfortably with both of your hands resting open, palms up.

2. Breathe comfortably and let your body relax,

3. Observe your thoughts, feelings and sensations and any sensory input from the present moment.

4. Allow everything to be exactly as it is and begin to mentally describe the present moment to yourself in the most positive way possible,

DAY 355

EYE AM HAPPY, HEALTHY, AND WHOLE

The eyes send messages to the brain that go beyond helping us see. The eyes integrate information into the left and right hemispheres of the brain and can be used to heal and prevent trauma, improve memory, and support integrating affirmations.

1. Sit comfortably with your eyes open and set a timer for five minutes.

2. With your head looking straight ahead, move your eyes to the left and to the right. Take about one second to go from one side to the next, continuing until the timer goes off.

3. Repeat the mantra, "I am happy, healthy, and whole."

4. Notice the thoughts and images that come to mind, continue repeating the mantra, believing it as honestly as you can.

DAY 356

LIGHT UP YOUR LIFE

Envision bright golden light radiating from deep within you and shining in all directions around you as you move throughout your day. Bring the light of kindness, the light of honesty and the light of compassion everywhere you go.

DAY 357

SURRENDER

"Try something different. Surrender."

- Rumi

DAY 358

MENTAL NOTING

One of the most difficult aspects of meditation is learning to embrace the multiple emotions that arise in the mind, as well as the distractions in the body and external atmosphere. Enable all to be just as it is when doing breath awareness meditation. Consider your current presence and surroundings to be the foreground of the conscious mind, and imagine that everything about you is a process of the unconscious mind sorting itself out.

DAY 359

AFFIRMATION FOR PRESENCE

"I am here, and I am awake now. I am here, and I am aware now, I am here and I am alive now."

DAY 360

ELEVATOR VISUALIZATION

1. Sit in a comfortable position and take a few deep breaths.

2. Visualize yourself stepping into an elevator with 33 floors.

3. Notice the buttons for each floor on the wall of the elevator, and watch as every button lights up as you make your way up to the 33rd floor.

4. Does the elevator stop at any other floors?

5. Does anyone else step into the elevator?

6. When you make it to the 33rd floor, what do you see?

DAY 361

NON ATTACHMENT BUCKET LIST

There is so much to do and look forward to in this world! Take some time today to consider all the adventures and experiences you'd like to have. Make a list of the extraordinary things you'd like to experience in this lifetime while maintaining a sense of non-attachment to whether any of them actually take place. I would love to experience _____ but my fulfilment and joy do not depend on it

DAY 362

LOVINGKINDNESS AND LEARNING

1. Sit comfortably with both your hands resting open, palms up

2. Breathe comfortably and let your body relax.

3. Cultivate stillness and a sense of lovingkindness

4. Bring your family and close loved ones to mind, sending them lovingkindness, silently asking "What can I learn from you?"

5. Bring your friends, neighbors, coworkers, and those with whom you have difficulty to mind, sending them lovingkindness, silently asking, “What can I learn from you?”

6. Breathe and listen for an answer before finishing your meditation.

DAY 363

SOCIAL MEDIA LOVE BOMBS

1. Visit social media accounts whose content supports, helps, or inspires you.

2. Post “love bomb” comments of gratitude and acknowledgement for the goodness being sent out into the universe.

3. Share the most inspiring, helpful, or supportive posts to your page or in direct messages to your friends and family members.

DAY 364

REFLECTION

The transformation of following your daily habits is almost complete you have taken such a leap of faith and now at this level are able to reflect on the journey.

Go back to your favorite habits you have marked or noted down as influential. These habits will become a part of your mantra as you reflect back on to what brings meaning and purpose into your life.

DAY 365

MOTIVATING FOR THE FUTURE

The future is nothing short of bright when we have our vision. The goal of life is not just look at the end goal but enjoy the journey. The rest of the book is a introduction into the rest of the factors that create resiliency to resolve issue.

Take this time and focus on what your goals are for Motivating for the future. List 3 things that you hold that will motivate you to accomplish your goals in any sense of the word. Motivate, inspire, and be a force of change. Practice taking 5 deep breaths and congratulate yourself for following your 365 Days. I hope it has had a profound impact on your life for the better.

Chapter 3

Daily Lifestyle and Success Habits

Daily habits to Learnza are about the lifestyle you need to create to live a meaningful life.

WAKE UP EARLY

In reality, a habit floats around a society, like a website floats around every other website, and it is widespread. The notion that we should learn to rise early. This is significant, but it is so passive that we dismiss it without delving deeply into its true significance. We can hear we need to get up early and go about our days without thinking about much else, but it will not sink in and become an actual practice because we will not have an actual technique to learn it. Try studying the quadratic formula without knowing what the term means, or using it mathematically; is it merely numbers and letters? We have no idea if we can learn a common pattern, including waking up early, and turn it into a habit that becomes a part of our routine and a part of our life to help us improve. This is where the "Learnza" technique comes into play; if you can

Learnza to wake up early, you understand the term; to wake up, you must be resting. It all starts at the bottom; we must form the habit by first comprehending the word. We must develop the habit of going to bed early to get as much rest as possible to wake up physically and mentally refreshed. The second aspect is the definition of waking up, which implies to begin waking up means to begin, because there can be no beginning without an end. So, if we want to wake up, we must finish our day if we are continuing previous feelings, philosophies, hurts, and traumas. Again, to be truly "woken," as my students put it, one must be authentic. If we do not, our days will be filled with the same challenges and anxiety stressors that we have yet to overcome. To be honest, we need to get rid of what was left over from the day before. It is here that the implementation process comes into play, as the prism of mathematics reveals, if we can take the word and comprehend its meaning, the application of genuinely waking will be a comb digital detox, a revitalized visit to what was once missing, and it was the dream that we were always expecting to be discovered.

SPACE MEETING

Examine our emotions. They move so fast that we are consuming digital content while falling into a social hierarchy in which we claim approval and "busy" ourselves every single minute of the day because that is how much time we have for meetings. We don't have time for anything else because our schedules are so packed. When I first hired my first assistant, Alex, he would schedule a "Room Meeting" in my calendar, forcing me to take a break from my hectic schedule. Alex did something very special for me that I now do on a regular basis. Again, that is the beauty of habits: they do not have to be the top six habits to cultivate in six weeks. Again, only successful treats from others that you can incorporate into your life, and this was the space meeting. This is not Elon Musk. Tesla or SpaceX fantasy meeting where we discuss space that will come later, I love exploring time and space but to get back on track the space meeting build space for yourself You devote 30 minutes to an hour per day to isolated meditation in a meeting that isn't even for you. Do you have time to take a break from work, not to engage with family or loved ones, or to do something that isn't allowing you to be alone directly? That is what the space meeting does, it gives you space, which is exactly what we desperately need and then lets you allow yourself to let go of any wasted time.

LETTING GO

Love for Yourself.

Validation for Yourself.

Acceptance for Everything You Are.

Gain the Love for Self.

Have Love for Yourself.

When looking for a partner, having a neutral mind set and energy is essential; this is not easy to achieve but can be achieved through years of practice. I've built a fan base of self-esteem and self-love that stems from emotional trauma and positive growth. Again, it all begins with you, so repeat

Myself.

Work.

Academic Life.

Partner.

CHOOSING A TRIGGER FOR YOUR MORNING ROUTINE

Getting started in the morning is the most important aspect of your day's productivity. As a result, you must exercise caution when selecting your morning triggers. Triggers are factors that cause you to act, similar to how the starter pistol at the start of a race signals runners that it is time to move.

Your morning triggers are simply the actions that prompt your habits, such as getting out of bed and brushing your teeth. How to Select Triggers

There are a few things to consider when you are selecting your morning routine triggers, for instance.

1. Morning triggers could be old habits. These old habits are already ingrained in your mind and may still be a part of your daily routine. You might have a habit of going to the bathroom at the same time every morning or doing laundry on the same days each week. These are known as habitual habits, and they must be understood in order to help prevent further harm.

2. Make certain that your triggers are simple to remember and execute. If you have to remind yourself of the triggers, it's a sign that they aren't working. Triggers should be automatic and require little to no thought, similar to how you automatically make a pot of coffee after brushing your teeth or a cup of chai; if you find yourself forgetting the habit, there is a good chance you have identified the incorrect trigger.

3. Remember any event or action can serve as a trigger for you. Triggers such as the end of your favorite newscast or the time you leave for work can be used. The trigger can be effective as long as it occurs on a daily basis. You should begin your morning routine as soon as you notice the triggers you've chosen for each day. You may need to keep a checklist for yourself for the first few weeks. Acting on your triggers will become second nature after this point.

REDUCE CHANCES OF FAILURE

When it comes to your morning routine, you are your own worst enemy. Set yourself up for success by making it easier for you to complete your morning tasks. Make sure you can do everything on your morning routine list in the shortest amount of time possible.

You can also go to bed early each night, so you will not take so long to get out of bed in the mornings. Products, software, or devices like a time management app or electric toothbrush can improve your life and make it easier to help you stick to your morning routine.

If a few days go by and you notice you cannot complete everything on your morning to compile a list, it is time to make adjustments. Do not put too many things on your list since this will frustrate you and keep you from sticking to your routine. Edit your morning routine until you can do everything on your list within the allotted time.

REWARD YOURSELF

To ensure that you stick to your morning routine, reward yourself when you complete everything on your list. Your "prizes" do not have to be anything too fancy. For instance, you can give yourself a few extra minutes of relaxation time or simply compliment yourself on a job well done. When you get instant gratification, you are making it easier to continue wholesome habits. Breaking your morning rituals' monotony by celebrating your accomplishments will keep you from getting off your routine. This will also help your productive habits to stick, which can help with time management and lower your stress and anxiety levels.

MODIFY YOUR HABITS AND IMPROVE YOUR LIFE

Habits can be your road to success or the key to your downfall. The choice is yours. Negative habits are often the toughest ones to let go of, so how about changing these negative ones and delivering them more positive? Positivity can change our perspective that is unlike anything imaginable. Thus, changing a habit requires conscious effort and dedication. In some fortunate instances, however, it is not willpower chance that spurs this change. Find the motivation to change your inner thoughts and accomplish the impossible.

If your goal is to lose 15 pounds but the Starbucks by your office or school is too tempting, it would be challenging to meet your goals. Who will say no to these delectable pastries and blonde expresso? A flavor becomes two bites, then ten. You've gained another five pounds without ever realizing it! Nonetheless, if desperation caused you to change jobs, taking your Starbucks south of your usual commute zone, you might have dropped three pounds without even attempting. Take a detour to extend the activities to involve identifying the broader perspective of thought outside the books. Determine not to consider the 25 pounds to be a larger amount. Actions and habits have a virtuous loop impact. When you sense the trigger, you act on it and applaud yourself, much as you might in a habit. The pastry shop was the catalyst of this situation, the ritual was entering the shop, and the pastry itself is the reward. By removing the stimulus, the routine and reward were separated from the sequence.

Unfortunately, eliminating the trigger is not so straightforward. It is only on rare instances that chasing influences ruin your life and cause dramatic change. Instead, resisting temptation is exhausting work! Since patterns are automatic, modifying them requires deliberate effort. You must formulate a strategy and have the resolve to adhere to it, no matter how daunting it is.

You do not consciously decide how many spoons of sugar to put in your morning coffee or chai, nor are you aware of biting your nails every time you are nervous. If you want to reach a particular goal, these are thoughts that might need to be changed. By becoming conscious of the problem, you can avoid acting on it consistently. Through repetition, your altered action will become a habit. Instead, it will soon become embedded in your subconscious, thereby changing the bad habit into a positive one. However, since habits are frequently formed without knowing, you must re-evaluate them regularly to see if you have picked up any new negative ones.

DEVISE A PLAN

The first step toward habit change is acceptance, followed by planning. To do this, determine how you want to change your existing habit, how it negatively affects you presently, and what you wish to achieve out of the change. Decide how you wish to achieve this objective and always keep a positive attitude.

Maybe your goal is to eat healthier. Grab a sheet of paper and write down your plan. Your plan may look something like this.

"I intend to consume healthy foods in order to achieve a healthier body for this." Instead of eating fast food on a regular basis, I would continue to consume fruits and vegetables. I'll sleep stronger, have more control, and have more endurance. This will enable me to complete more work, spend more time with my baby, and feel happier." This is your strategy, your dedication to progress.

This blueprint becomes a vision for yourself in the future. The Law of Attraction, on the other hand, says it all. You may accomplish your goals by visualizing and wishing for them. Good thinking is often associated with the positive mind.

Famous personalities including Lady Gaga, Oprah, Barak, Obama practice this art of the method of the Laws of Attraction, and they have recommended using a vision board. Instead of merely envisioning your goals in your mind, place them in front of you. It is a whiteboard, a corner of the wall, or even a refrigerator where you place specific items, phrases, or anything that helps you focus on your goal. Suppose your goal is to stop consuming harmful substances, thereby reminding yourself of your ultimate aim. By observing this daily, you will feel increasingly encouraged to achieve it.

TRACKING YOUR HABITS

Even as you try to make a change, try keeping a journal to record the harmful habit. Take, for example, that you want to stop drinking too much coffee. Record every cup of coffee with a note in a journal or a smartphone. You will need to create multiple columns to keep careful tabs on your habit.

An example of the column titles and what such a journal entry may look like is shown below.

Date and Time: Tuesday, 23rd March, 10:00 AM

Emotional State Before the Behavior: sleepy and stressed

Physical State Before the Behavior: At the cafe outside the office

Frequency and Duration of the Behavior: 2 cups of coffee so far

Emotional State After Behavior: Relaxed and wide awake

As you strive hard to change, you may notice a shift in its frequency within a week. By noting the trigger, sleepiness, and stress, you can begin thinking about a constructive method for replacing the behavior with more acceptable behavior.

SET GOALS

Aside from the vision, long and short-term objectives are important. Your long-term aim is to lose the weight and hold it off. You can also mention targets such as "reduced cholesterol," and "reduced blood pressure" However, it may be difficult to achieve.

Instead, strive for a target of losing 10 pounds over two weeks and 20 at the end of the month. Small steps lead to big achievements. So your final goal doesn't have to be daunting and challenging to accomplish. Really, it will be okay to keep track of your achievements, make yourself a list and cross things off one by one Any achievement will increase your trust.

BELIEVE AND COMMIT

Although dedication is required for any plan to succeed, confidence is also required. If you remain unsure, continually in doubt, and challenge your own progress, chances are you will abandon the

commitment you made, which could result in a release when you decide you can not accomplish your target, that it seems impossible.
Believe in yourself and you can't do anything else. Have faith in your ability to achieve your goal; only then can you commit to completing it fully. Psychologists have shown that believing is a critical factor in success, and the vision board listed earlier will assist you in instilling that belief in yourself.
Keep in mind that habits never die as long as the cause is present.

A habit, like learning to ride a bike, is never forgotten once established. It cannot be lost because it becomes rooted in your subconscious. You may, however, alter it. Change the habit to suit your life and ambitions, and then use it to your advantage. When nervousness hits, you may want to continue chewing your nails, but instead, occupy your fingers with something else, such as twirling your hair or writing down why you are nervous.

Old habits are more difficult to break, so aim to catch them early. You could be forming a retail obsession, whether you choose to shop while you are depressed or not satisfied. Stop it before the situation worsens. Spend the buying energy on something else rather than accumulating a pile of credit card debt. Keep in mind that routines, including those broken, have the potential to resurface. If the prior triggers and stimuli are added, an ex-smoker will still smoke! Pick up a smoke and relapse into this heinous habit. To maintain the changed habit, you must be aware of the reasons! While smoking is more of an obsession than a habit, the rules for dealing with this addiction remain the same, so let's look at ways we can replace bad habits with good ones.

HABIT SWAPPING

If you want to overcome your negative behavior, you must learn how to replace bad habits with good ones. We've seen that recognizing triggers makes rerouting behavior simple, but it's also important to find a new behavior to follow that increases the trigger and response.

Eliminating a trigger can be difficult because most of the time it is something conventional, such as a need for comfort, being tired, feeling upset, or even being with someone in a specific location. However, there is something you can do, and that is to change the way you respond to triggers. To do so, you must first learn how to replace negative habits with positive ones.

Primarily, you must decide whether you want a total or partial swap that can be increased over time. This is dependent on your personality and habits, so be completely honest with yourself about whether you can manage switching habits.

To be creative, there are no “wrong” or “right” swaps, but it is recommended that you focus on swaps that seem logical to you. For example, if you want to break the habit of eating candy because it is bad for your health, replacing it with sunflower seeds will be much easier than going for a jog around the block. I enjoy deciphering my snacks for keto-friendly snacks. The idea is the same. I'm still eating crunchy and savory snacks, but switching them around gives me a better idea of what I can handle.

If you want to successfully replace a negative habit with a positive one, you must ensure that the latter makes you feel rewarded. If it does not, it will simply not work, and you will quickly revert to your old negative habits. As a result, avoid substituting candy for vegetables, especially if you despise them. Choose a healthy snack replacement that makes you feel rewarded and that you genuinely enjoy.

REWARDING?

Below are some excellent examples of positive swaps and the numerous benefits they provide. If you're stuck for ideas, you could even try some of these:

If you want to quit smoking but don't know what to do, how about replacing it with exercise? The good news is that exercising not only makes you look better but also significantly improves your health. You get immediate health benefits as well as a distraction from your smoking habit. Whether it's a lap at the local pool, a jog around the lake, or some cardio, exercising improves your health and serves as a great habit replacement that can easily help you quit smoking.

When it comes to food swaps, most people remember the flavor, but they overlook an important detail — the texture of the food. This means you may be addicted to the crunch of the potato chips rather than the chips themselves. Other crunchy snacks, such as popcorn, crackers, or nuts, should be considered as alternatives. One principal point to remember is that unhealthy foods should always be replaced with healthier alternatives, as this is an important part of the habit-breaking process.

You must make an effort to identify the root causes and replace destructive habits with constructive ones. The reduction in psychological tension is indescribable. In addition, by incorporating an incentive scheme into your swap, you can quickly eliminate unhealthy habits, boost your self-esteem, and take control of your life.

CHANGE ENVIRONMENT?

You can also try changing your environment in addition to all of these habit-changing methods. Most habits are triggered by our environment; changing it can help you avoid your habit. Changing your environment does not have to imply relocating or quitting your job or career (though it certainly could mean that). It could be as simple as moving your chair, incorporating in-between workout exercises off the patio, or not keeping sweets in the house. It could imply relocating your television so that it is not visible from the table where you eat dinner, if you do not want the family to watch Netflix while they eat. Changing your environment can also mean not hanging out with people who share your bad habits and thus encourage them.

TIPS ON HOW TO DEAL WITH YOUR HABIT TRIGGERS

#1. Identify the Trigger: The first task here is to recognize the habit triggers, which will prove you are successful with the mindfulness process. The identifying trigger also helps you know how to deal with them to avoid it the next time.

#2. Disrupt the Trigger: After recognizing the trigger, you will now need to take immediate actions to sabotage it. If you delay, the habitual behavior might take root for the long run. The faster you can disrupt the trigger, the more likely you are to avoid the habitual behavior.

#3. Come up with an Alternative: If you end up engaging in your habitual behavior, you can find alternatives to deal with the situation. Identify what happened, why it happened, and find ways of dealing with the habit trigger better next time. Even though you end up engaging in the habitual behavior, you can be sure of avoiding it next time if you find an alternative ahead of time.

#4. Encourage Yourself on Your Achievements: When you manage to disrupt the habit trigger and successfully avoid the habitual behavior, you should be happy and record your progress. You can note down what happened, what you did about it, and why it was successful.

#5. Repeat the Process: The key to countering the triggers is by being consistent. For that, you should repeat the entire trigger evasion progress. This will make it easier, and you will naturally know when a trigger can occur and deal with it before it leads to a habit.

ADMIT YOU SLID BACK, AND IT'S OK!

AVOID BEATING YOURSELF UP

Setbacks do not always imply that you are a failure or a loser when it comes to breaking a habit. It simply means you are a human being. Stopping a bad habit is a process, which means it may not be easy. Try not to be too hard on yourself. Record what you messed up and how you intend to avoid repeating, habitual behavior in the future to avoid future setbacks.

When beginning a new habit, keep a positive attitude because it will help you forge a path forward even when things appear difficult. Every setback teaches you about your flaws, who you are, and how to avoid them in the future.

The "one step at a time" approach will make changing your habit easier. When viewed as a whole, the change may appear to be a huge burden or responsibility, but when viewed as a single step at a time, you will be better off.

Chapter 4

Motivation: A Narrative Story

STILLNESS

“Hamza, what if I’m never cool?” he wondered. “I don’t fit into any clique, and I don’t play any sports; I’m useless.” He couldn’t say what others thought of him as they passed him in the corridor, but they had no idea about his abilities. He was driven to undo the damage done to his reputation as a result of a brief high school experience. In my self-esteem seminars, I enjoy asking the audience questions. When people consider asking a question in front of the crowd, I still note their painfully adolescent expressions of self-consciousness on their faces.

This habit of caring more about what other people think about our thoughts than we do about our own thoughts usually begins in high school, but it can last a lifetime. It is time to be careful of what we are doing and, in essence, to graduate from high school. It is time to return to my pre-high school days of naive creativity and relational fearlessness and reflect on my former self. Again, the core persona that we must create and internalize is the self. Most people are unaware of how easily they can develop the social emotions they crave. Instead, they live as if they are still! Teenagers listening to other people's fictitious judgments is a fallacy. They end up planning their lives based on what other people think of them. Nonetheless, we should break the habit. "Why should the way I feel be determined by the feelings in someone else's head?" Emerson enquired.

DEEPER CONNECTIONS

"People notice a change in your attitude but do not notice their behavior that made you change it."

- Lao-tzu -

LIVE, LOVE, LEARNZA

Motivate students by building strong, trust-based relationships with your people.

"People living deeply," wrote 20th-century author Anais Nin, "Have no fear of death. "Any years ago,

I was consulting with a Texas high school, and I was allowed to identify the best ways to innovate students.

It all goes back to the foundation of the Learnza philosophy which is creating a pedagogical space that allows students to move from one object to another. By teaching students to move from one task to another, they can understand their particular position and create more far-reaching results. The positive effects that arise from introducing a pedagogical approach are infinite. Regardless of how technically advanced, the teachings methodology may be the best approach to teach multicultural students effectively. Again, people living deeply have the inspiration to change; thus, there must be a robust pedagogical space to teach and impact.

As I visualized each friend and relative coming to visit me, I had to speak to them out loud. I had to say to them what I wanted them to know as I was dying. As I spoke to my loved ones, I could not help breaking down. I was filled with such a sense of loss. It was not my own life, and I was mourning. It was the love I had lost. Alternatively, to be more exact, a lost communication of Love. I got to see how much I had left out of my life. How many beautiful feelings I had about my children, for example, that I'd never explicitly expressed? At the end of the exercise, I was an emotional mess. I had rarely cried that hard in my life. However, when those emotions cleared, a wonderful thing happened. I was clear. I knew what was important to me and who mattered. From that day on, I vowed not to leave anything to chance. I made up my mind never to leave anything unsaid. I wanted to live as if I might die any moment. The entire experience altered the way.

Moreover, the exercise's significant point was not lost on me: *We do not have to wait until we are actually near death to receive these benefits of perception of truly living.* We can create the experience internally. A few years later, when my aunt Dr. Naila was lying suffering in a hospital in Minnesota due to stage 4 pancreatic cancer, I could not rush to her side to repeat to her all the love and gratitude I felt for who she had been for me. In Mecca, on pilgrimage, I was with my mother, and that was how I made my peace with her death. When she died, my grieving was intense but fleeting due to me being able to forgive myself in Mecca and Medina. In a matter of days, I believed everything necessary about my aunt had entered into me and would live there as a loving spirit forever.

POWER LOAD MARGIN THEORY

My life's philosophy and work revolves around teaching, learning, and implementing the Power Load Margin (PLM) Theory. Throughout the research and findings of Howard McCluskey I shifted the research of Learnza to help young adults age throughout the lifespan. Combining the theory of margin to understand adult life as they grow older is valuable information that guides successful aging through the lifespan. Combining the theory of margin, specifically the power load margin theory, can be practical to verify that M equals L divided by P or power helps individuals with their responsibilities. This theory aims to show the power factors, and power itself is a robust set of skills and contingencies that can help anyone succeed.

Since Power equals resources, and Load equals demands and margins. The 1963 theory talks about the power-load-margin (PLM) measure of how many resources (power) the learner must offer. The learner must offset the demands (Load) then. The Power of Life Margin is essential to the mental health of the adult and young adults alike. The PLM theory allows the person to invest in life expansion projects and experiences, including learning experiences. A low margin indicates the adult is under stress or illness, not fulfilling their potential (Stevenson, 1982).

Specifically, this theory has not been examined in the realm of motivational coaching and life coaching. For the war, I am buying this theory with the fundamental principles of resiliency training through motivational interviewing, which will help individuals reclaim what they have lost and overcome difficult situations. Specifically, again, this can help with young adults dealing with the burnout experience. Thus, in conclusion setting is critical when implemented early enough in student's education, motivational coaching in the learning community (Legg et al., 2018).

"Effective coaching distributes leadership and keeps the focus on teaching and learning. A highly effective, comprehensive coaching program in a school or district supports coaches to systematically gather various evidence to illustrate the impact of coaching on teachers, administrators, and students"

- Van Nieuwerburgh (2018 p. 13)

Additionally, the bond between a mentor and mentee helps alleviate burnout and helps students emotionally focus on coping skills.

This study will focus on this valuable relationship between the mentor and mentee. The focus of the study is to share the student's perspective of motivational coaching. Moreover, the purpose is to highlight student experiences.

Strategies for motivational coaching currently on the market involve life coaching under a mentor's supervision to counsel and encourage individuals with career and life challenges (Newnham-Kansas et al., 2011). Coaches are successful when they have students maintain a balance between self-esteem, nutrition, and physical activity.

One way to ease yourself into self-motivation is to act as if you were the laziest person on the planet. Accepting that you will do your task slowly and lazily, there is no anxiety or dread about getting it started. You can even have fun by entering into it as if you were in a slow-motion comedy, flowing into the job like a person composed of water. Nevertheless, the irony is the slower you start something, the faster you will be finished. When you first think about doing something challenging and overwhelming, you are most aware of how you do not want to do it at all. In other words, the mental picture you have of this activity, of doing it fast and furiously, is not appropriate.

So, you think of ways to avoid doing the job altogether. Thinking about starting slowly is straightforward. Moreover, doing it slowly allows you actually to start doing it. Therefore, it gets finished. Another thing that happens when you flow into a project slowly is that speed will often overtake you without forcing it. Precisely the natural rhythm inside you will get you in "sync" with what you are doing. You will be surprised how soon your conscious mind stops "forcing" the action, and your unconscious mind supplies you with tranquil energy.

MY STORY

SOUL SEARCHING

I was not born with a silver spoon in my mouth and had to work hard for the majority of my life to get where I am now. Even the best of us go on journeys, and mine was always focused on discovering my soul. I was thinking to myself, such as, “Where is my life going?” What allows me to be content? Will I ever be able to make enough money to support myself? What does it mean to be alive? I hustled my way through corporate America and am always looking for my Zen spot. I began my life coaching practice in order to maintain a Zen state of mind, but I struggled to discover my soul.

I wanted to advance my career and make more money when I was younger, so that was my motivation for breaking out of the rut. I was concerned that I would find a snag at work and wished to be more enthusiastic about it. I also desired to begin actively saving and investing. During my soul-searching, I recall thinking that I didn’t have much of a reason not to press harder because my parents still worked hard to provide a better life for my brother and me, despite getting even less than I did at my age.

My parents taught me that there is very little in life that is handed to you. If you really want something, you must go out and get it. I soon began networking in Dallas, recalling what I had learned. I have started a personal project outside of my 9-to-5, drafting possibilities for my book and how to make the most of your 20s. In November 2018, I launched Learnza, LLC, marking a landmark moment in both my professional and personal lives. The difficulty was not in discovering my soul, but in understanding how my soul was my passion. My life and soul are inextricably linked. I'm writing this because I'm thinking about how fluid I live my life, with my passion, heart, and soul all at the same time.

Finally, you must make a mental, physical, and spiritual commitment to your objectives. Consider how your life will be. What are your thoughts? The target must leave your head and invade your senses, spirit, and being. Visualization is the term for this. As a consequence, performance is contingent on this manifestation.

Of course, you don't have to go to the Bahamas to overcome target ambivalence or indecision (although the end beaches and crystal-clear waters are a nice touch). I could have quickly been energized after a weekend spent at home, running, reading, and talking about my problems with family and close friends. Everyone has an approach that works best for them. The main thing is that you feel the drive and need to step forward and accomplish your goals, and that you are prepared to work hard and do whatever it takes to do so.

Don't allow yourself to become depressed. The aim is to build a viable goal on which you can concentrate and produce results in the near future. If you set goals that apply from now until eternity, go for it, knowing that you might change your mind later in life. What are your expectations for the next five years, based on where you are now and where you want to be? To reply, you must first understand who you are, what kind of life you want, and try to concentrate on the positive (while being realistic).

UNEXPECTED OPPORTUNITIES

PUTTING THE LEARNZA METHODS TO THE TEST

When I left my job to start Learnza, LLC in 2017, (or the idea of a motivational coaching company that factors in the student above all else). I struggled and relied on friends and family while saving for two months in order to apply for a start-up fund. It was the most difficult period of my life. I'd never felt so hopeless before, but it aided in the development of my GRIT. I would work 90 hours a week and learned not to cry, because this was my goal: to fight through the struggle and recognize the greater purpose, not just believe in myself. I've spoken at 15+ Learnza, LLC events as July 1st, 2019 approaches. I am very involved in DFW community fundraisers, charity events, and, most importantly, collaboration with WeWork and, most recently, Industrious. I hope my incredible journey inspires anyone who has realized they are not prepared for the challenges of being an entrepreneur. In summary, here are some suggestions to assist those in need:

• Evaluate your actions. It is critical to remember that your attitudes are influenced by your own culture and mental state. If you have a negative reaction to a situation, identify the source of your stress and remove yourself from the situation.

• Become acquainted with yourself. The most important gift we can give ourselves is self-love.

• Create a judgment-free zone in your life. Do not pass judgment on anyone based on how they live or choose to live their lives. As a result, you will not feel the pressure that others are judging you.

• Be flexible. Be adaptable in any difficult situation. Make short-term victories, "Creating short-term victories differs from hoping for short-term victories. The former is passive, while the latter is active "(Kotter, 2012 p. 12).

• Be sure to include yourself. Include yourself in whatever makes you happy, whether you are introverted or extroverted.

My life has not been easy, and I have learned the true meaning of struggle, success, and ambition since that day. My trials and tribulations have compelled me to confront my own beliefs. During this time, I became increasingly convinced that the five philosophies I had established five years prior to founding Learnza LLC would see me through this difficult period and keep me on track to achieve all of my objectives. I shared these points of view because I adore being a guide for anyone struggling to find their place in life, society, and beyond.

Philosophy 1: When it comes to your career, find the one that sparks your interest. You must be self-starting, determined, and never consider yourself to be in a job. Consider yourself in a complex role in society. As a result, you must maintain some control over your income. Having multiple income streams allows you to express your true desires and opens up a world of opportunities. Think creatively at times, and always find value in your experiences to help you get to the next step.

Philosophy 2: I, like 10% of the US workforce at the time, could now attest that a full-time job was no guarantee. As a result, you must hope for

the best while bracing for the worst. If you can't afford your current lifestyle while working toward your long-term goals with one job, you'll need a second or third. Do not be afraid of the struggle it will only make you better!

Philosophy 3: The more work you have, the more work you get done. Having a few jobs kept me busy while also allowing me to stay organized and responsible.

Philosophy 4: Do what makes you happy; work hard and trust that the money will come. Understand your worth and honestly assess your strengths. If you believe you are getting a raw deal from the massive cheese and nothing else, speak up and seek change.

CONCLUSION

In summary, I was born in Lahore, Pakistan, and grew up there until the age of four, when my father struggled and worked for years before bringing my mother and me to the United States in the 1990s. In the tiny town of Omaha, Nebraska, I was fortunate to grow up in a loving home. Because of the hard hardships we had to face growing up in our Texas climate, we were taught the habits of mindfulness at a youthful age. Growing up was easy; however, when it came time to find my identity, I was challenged. What I ended up developing was a genuine sense of leadership. Strategy, leadership, capital and skills, initiative management, and community are examples of these. I wrote this book so individuals can learn how to practice daily habits for an entire year to become more mindful. Becoming mindful leads to resiliency to change and then can motivate students to become better. They can seek acceptance, garner patience, and become grateful for the hurdles that they have had to overcome. Thus, compassion and grace are the forefront for change to practice and "learn" the daily habits to Learnza.

Learnza workers all have a vested interest in working on the procedures listed by accomplished corporate leaders, thus assisting organizations all over the globe in achieving their particular priorities and objectives. Ahmed Hassan, the chief of our global operations team, has recognized the influence that few leaders do, which is why he is the most visible representation of heart-centered leadership. Leading from excellent to exceptional should not include coming up with solutions and then inspiring everyone to pursue the messianic quest. It entails being humble enough to accept something you do not yet understand" (Pelicer, 2008, p. 12).

Exploring the interaction between educational coaching and students, which I nurture at Learnza, I might create a study issue that deals with students' academic achievement pressure, which causes them to be overcome with tension and anxiety. This contributed to the conclusion of my doctoral study at Baylor University. The study indicates that educators and parents place a lot of strain on their pupils. The inconsistencies in the proof. Through drawing inferences from the literature on the validity of hypotheses applicable to Educational Coaching (EC). The EC provides significant academic opportunities to students and works with them to demonstrate meaningful lifelong learning. The study's specific goal was to investigate exactly how to develop mindfulness and reliance. This is the curriculum I will introduce to Camp Learnza. Camp Learnza has always been a vision of mine to support the underprivileged and undeserved in rural areas around the world. We are very proud of our squad, both at home and abroad. The first inauguration day will be celebrated on February 28th, 2021 in Islamabad, Pakistan.

The students embody the demographics of the community, and school climates and structures around Pakistan can help form the narratives that will be gathered across five 90-minute interviews with each individual and thematic review. The analysis of narratives shows these students' living experiences as well as our workings through

Learnza and the teachers rotating around concepts of (1) The Professional Self, (2) Curriculum Leadership/Educational Coaching, and (3) Mindfulness. Most students are pursuing secondary science education as a second career but remain dedicated to the field. "There will be moments when we will slip and crash, and other times when we will become so completely disoriented that we will momentarily lose our path." We must bear in mind that it is more about the trip, not the end" (Pelicer, 2008, p.10). True mindfulness and true leadership benefit from the production of true skills. Standing faithful to one's purpose and objective makes it worthwhile to engage in this mindfulness process of self-discovery, expansion, and progress in order to genuinely feel inspired and self-worth.

THE END

Bibliography

Chandler, S. (2012). *100 ways to motivate yourself: Change your life forever*. Red Wheel/Weiser.

Cohen, P. A., Kulik, J. A., & Kulik, C. L. C. (1982). Educational outcomes of tutoring: A meta-analysis of findings. *American Educational Research Journal*, *19*(2), 237–248. https://doi.org/10.3102/00028312019002237

Cornett, J., & Knight, J. (2009). Research on coaching. In J. Knight (Ed.), *Coaching:*

Approaches and perspectives (pp. 192–216). Corwin Press.

Creswell, J. W., & Poth, C. N. (2018). *Qualitative inquiry and research design: Choosing among 5 approaches* (4th ed.). Sage.

DeFeo, D. J., & Caparas, F. (2014). Tutoring as transformative work: A phenomenological case study of tutors' experiences. *Journal of College Reading and Learning*, *44*(2), 141–163. https://doi.org/10.1080/10790195.2014.906272

Dukes, S. (1984). Phenomenological methodology in the human sciences. *Journal of Religion and Health*, *23*(3), 197–203. https://doi.org/10.1007/BF00990785

Kotter, J. P. (2012). *Leading change*. Harvard Business Press.

Legg, E., Newland, A., & Bigelow, R. (2018). Somebody's eyes are watching: The impact of coaching observations on empowering motivational climates and positive youth development. *Journal of Park and*

Recreation Administration, *36*(4), 90–106. https://doi.org/10.18666/JPRA-2018-V36-I4-8885

McBath, G. L. (2019). *Evaluating the interconnectivity between Self-Determination Theory and undergraduates' volunteer cessation: An empirical, philosophical phenomenological study* (Pre-Dissertation Concept Paper with Annotated Bibliography).

Newnham-Kanas, C., Morrow, D., & Irwin, J. D. (2011). Participants' perceived utility of motivational interviewing using co-active life coaching skills on their struggle with obesity. *Coaching: An International Journal of Theory, Research and Practice*, *4*(2), 104–122. https://doi.org/10.1177/0009922891030007066

Patton, M. Q. (2002). *Variety in qualitative inquiry: Qualitative research and evaluation methods* (3rd ed.). Sage.

Showers, B., & Joyce, B. (1996). The evolution of peer coaching. *Educational Leadership*, *53*(6), 12–16.

Simanca, F., Gonzalez Crespo, R., Rodríguez-Baena, L., & Burgos, D. (2019). Identifying students at risk of failing a subject by using learning analytics for subsequent customized tutoring. *Applied Sciences*, *9*(3), 1–17. https://doi.org/10.3390/app9030448

Stevenson, J. S. (1982). Construction of a scale to measure load, power, and margin in life. *Nursing Research, 31*(4), 222–225. https://doi.org/10.1097/00006199-198207000-00009

Tebb, S. (1995). An aid to empowerment: A caregiver well-being scale. *Health & Social Work*, *20*(2), 87–92. https://doi.org/10.1093/hsw/20.2.87

van Nieuwerburgh, C. (2018). *Coaching in education: Getting better results for students, educators, and parents*. Routledge.

Wood, D., Bruner, J. S., & Ross, G. (1976). The role of tutoring in problem solving. *Journal of Child Psychology and Psychiatry*, *17*(2), 89–100. https://doi.org/10.1111/j.1469-7610.1976.tb00381.x

Yasin, M. A. S. M., & Dzulkifli, M. A. (2011). Differences in depression, anxiety and stress between low-and high-achieving students. *Journal of Sustainability Science and Management*, *6*(1), 169–178.

Made in the USA
Coppell, TX
03 July 2021